To my Grandson Richard
from Gran

20-11-97

Eternal Words

Edited by

Andrew Head

First published in Great Britain in 1997 by
POETRY NOW
1-2 Wainman Road, Woodston,
Peterborough, PE2 7BU
Telephone (01733) 230746
Fax (01733) 230751

All Rights Reserved

Copyright Contributors 1997

HB ISBN 1 86188 735 3
SB ISBN 1 86188 720 5

FOREWORD

Although we are a nation of poetry writers we are accused of not reading poetry and not buying poetry books: after many years of listening to the incessant gripes of poetry publishers, I can only assume that the books they publish, in general, are books that most people do not want to read.

Poetry should not be obscure, introverted, and as cryptic as a crossword puzzle: it is the poet's duty to reach out and embrace the world.

The world owes the poet nothing and we should not be expected to dig and delve into a rambling discourse searching for some inner meaning.

The reason we write poetry (and almost all of us do) is because we want to communicate: an ideal; an idea; or a specific feeling. Poetry is as essential in communication, as a letter; a radio; a telephone, and the main criteria for selecting the poems in this anthology is very simple: they communicate.

Poetry is a form of communication which has been around for many years. Poetry was once very popular but slowly, people's interest in it has diminished and many people gave it a stereotypical image of being boring and believing that poets themselves were usually bizarre individuals.

But today, in the 1990s poetry is becoming increasingly popular with more and more poets coming out of the closet. Poetry is now generally accepted my most as a talent which requires skill, imagination and creativity.

'Eternal Words' is a collection of poetry written by the poets of the 90s. This anthology shows how talented the poets are proving to the readers that poetry is not just some age old past-time. The poems vary in style and form, touching upon many issues, both modern and traditional. 'Eternal Words' shows us that poetry is something which should be appreciated by everyone.

Contents

The River Way	Clive Weston Sirett	1
An Unforgettable Night	A K Guest	2
It Could Be You	Bob Boyd	3
Save Our City!	Fiona Root	4
Finding Me	Tina Dix	4
Whistlestop	Margaret Rose	5
Water Time	David Hazlett	6
Rain	B L R Jones	7
Oppressed	Rhieanon Miles	7
A Change Of Scene	Mary Anne Scott	8
Dear Daddy	D M Bancroft	9
Night Terrors	Christina Ledwith	10
Darkness	Ryan Hooper	11
Time	Eileen Gerrish	11
Memories Of An Immigrant - 'The Four Seasons'	Gloria Aldred Knighting	12
The Garden	C Briggs	13
Only A Number	Elizabeth A Hutchison	14
Love	E Smith	14
Ice Maiden	Stacey Davis	15
Reflections	Deana Houghton	16
Dear Mum	Finola Crudden	17
A Miner's Tale	Muriel M McLeod	18
No Restrictions	V Fazacherley	19
I Care Just As You	Mike Lakey	20
I Wonder	Patricia Andrews	20
Seashore	Win Dukelow	21
Fear	Jean Hollings Grant Ross	22
Dreams	Larry Bowen	22
The Lady Of The Lake	Michele Glazer	23
Untitled	Tracey Rush	24
Been Lonely	Janine Dickinson	24
Resolution Of An Artist	Alastair Buchanan	25
Little Blue Bear	Ka Lunnon	26
Together Again	Melvyn Roiter	26

Remember Me	Joan Rastall	27
Nocturne	John Davies	28
The Return Of The Swallow	Finola Crudden	29
The Industrial Waste	Angela Speyers	30
Our Valley's Bus Route To Romance	Charles Ivor Morris	31
Love Is	Amanda-Lea Manning	32
Unwanted Gift	Sue Allison	33
Traffic Jam	Rosline Allen Gayle	34
A Beginning	A Carrigan	34
Pathetic Parent	Timothy Alexander	35
Sometimes	C McAloon	36
Instincts	Jean Tennent Mitchell	37
Losing You	Thomas C Ryemarsh	38
Sketches	William Price	38
A School	Basma Tafsirullah	39
Moments	Delia Marheinshe	40
Rebirth	Phoenix J Martin	41
Bleating	Tess Bates	42
Harmony	Margaret J Franklin	43
The 30s Crowd On Saturday Night	Celia Turner	44
Tears	Maria Tangen	45
To Stress	Anne Mackle	46
The Swallow	Christine Conway	46
Nature's Gifts	E M Dolphin	47
The Last Rose Of Summer	Michael Creed	48
Come Back	Lyn Cabble	48
When Liam Met Lennon	Angela White	49
The Poet's Song	D M Gale	50
Now I Walk With Him	Hazel P Marsay	50
Fantasy	Mary Hulme	51
In The Still Of The Night	Belinda Pyett	52
Africa's Bush	Diandra Glazer	52
Good-Bye	Ann Maurie	53
Signs Of Spring	Kathleen Speed	54

Head Sailor	K Latham Grimes	54
Letting Go	Doris Holland	55
Rainbow	Kate Douglas	56
Ebb And Flow	Clive W Macdonald	56
True Love	Win Davies	57
The Prisoner	Stephanie Hulley	58
Love Is	Polly Cox	59
Incline Of Day	Lee Laidlaw	60
Friend	Mary Jo West	61
The Cuckoo	A E Doney	62
If Our Eyes Could Only Speak	D S Arthur	63
No Distance Between Us	Donna Dudley	63
Wedding Blues	Barbara Pickles	64
Summer's Day	Patrick Humble	64
Weekend Away	Rob Baston	65
Silence	B Baker	66
Spirit Of The Eagle	C M Bellamy	66
Top Withins	Justin Barnard	67
Fellow Traveller	Norma Cohen	68
Once Your Wife	Deana Houghton	69
Untitled	C E Cannon	70
Quietness	Edith Meldrum Cooke	70
Faith	Colin Hush	71
To Live One Day On Earth	Sam Royce	72
When You're Gone	Joanne Ramsden	73
Social Classes	Tay Collicutt	74
The Wind's Discordant Ball	Ken Ford	75
Gap Bridging The World	H G Griffiths	76
Be Patient	Julie Allwright	76
Mexico City	Olga Kenyon	77
Home-Made Wine	Yvonne Smith	78
Moving On	Lesley Kate Mitchell	78
What Is A Soul?	Elsa M Summers	79

Reflections	Denis Holgate	80
Heads High, As The Orchestra Played Till The End	Katie Prentice	81
Together Again	Melvyn Roiter	82
The Meadows	M Parnell	82
Max's Mop	Dawn Potter	83
Jordan	Irene Di Mascio	84
Empty I Am	Paul Hetherington	85
The Better Way	William Price	86
The Mother And Child Relationship	K A Davis	86
More Respect	Antonio Martorelli	87
Who?	Fitzlillian	88
The World Cup Regatta, Munich, June 1977	Marie Barker	88
Happy Birthday Juliet	James Thomas Hopkins	89
Never Let It Happen Again	Christine Davis	90
Anger Trapped	Ellen Cooper	91
Womanhood	K J Herbert	92
Work Together	Alan Green	92
I Believe In This Earth	Jack Allerston	93
I M - R S Thomas	Andrew Hawthorne	94
The Palaces Of The Anti Hero	Mark Hemingway	94
First Love	Zahra Lalani	95
Death Of Innocence	Dionne Lindsay	96
Self-Psychoanalysis	Keith Murdoch	97
A Thought For Today	Bernadette C Curran	97
Eye In The Sky	Stephen Gyles	98
The Blood-Red Hand	Kim Montia	99
Every	Andy McPheat	100
The Green - Cambridge Early Spring	Elizabeth Hampden	101
Divine . . .	Suzanne Woolner	101
Terrestrial Shells	Elizabeth Ashworth	102

Workless	A Smart	102
Richard III		
At The Film Society	F L Bramah	103
Shattered	Anne-Marie Whitwell	104
A Way Out	Kim Harrison	105
Acacia Avenue	G C Freeth	106
Spin Doctor	Duncan Campbell	106
House Of God	Tony Jones	107
The Downside		
Of Democracy!	Barbara J Parsons	108
And There Was Love	Tony Jones	109
Nunc Dimittis	B J Bramwell	110
First Kiss	Amanda Lawrence	110
Aliens	Robert Godfrey	111
The Dream	Jeremy Gadd	112
The Peace Of Sinking		
Your Head In The Bath	Ross Styants	113
Charred	Michael Kemp	114
Love Is The Key	David Brade	116
Time Passes	Daniel Laverty	116
At The End Of The Day	Des Billington	117
Love Of Our Life	R M Campbell	118
Do You Love Me?	Amanda Lawrence	119
A Spring Flower	J Cuthbert	119
Full Moon Friday	Cath Simpkins	120
Life Is Like Geometry!	Susan Oliver	121
He Never Went Back	Richard Clewlow	122
First Wave	Glenn Freeth	123
Tears	E Shirley Whitman	123
Number 7	Jason Roycroft	124
A Journey	Tom Clarke	125
Jelly Beans	Victoria Buckley	126
By My Side	Ceryn Rowntree	127
When It All Adds Up	Anne Melling	128

THE RIVER WAY

Let's go the river way to school she said,
For six years I knew the names of all the insects
On that warm summer towpath,
And she knew all the flowers.
Many a morning we were late for the register
Having watched a dragonfly or two emerge . . .
On a shuddering reed stem.
There would never be anything to separate us,
Except The Eleven Plus.

Five years passed . . .
The river, with my hopes, rose and fell,
Washing away a wooden bridge,
Then . . .
Suddenly I saw her at the autumn fairground,
I froze . . .
Summer towpaths swam before me,
I called out 'Gina, Gina!' but my plea was drowned
By the din of the Dodgems,
And Bobby Darin's 'Dream Lover, Where Are You'?

A hand reached out to her . . .
In a spike-heeled twist of oily turf,
And a swirl of pink gingham lace
She was gone . . . lost in the crowd.
I was just like Buddy Holly then,
But he was like the Everly Brothers
Both of them!
After the fair had closed
I walked the silent towpath,
And remembered the names of all the insects.

Clive Weston Sirett

An Unforgettable Night

Coming home from work one
Stormy night,
as the snow lay on the
Ground
The wind was howling round
my ears, as I was homeward
Bound.

As I came towards my
Bus stop,
An old man I did
espy
His clothes were old and
Ragged,
and I heard a mournful
Cry.
I stood and listened, and
Then I heard, his sobbing
voice in the rain,
God has taken my lovely
Wife
whom I will never
See again.

I have neither friends or
Relations God,
and I don't want my lonely
life,
There is only one thing left
for me, and that is
Suicide.
I could not let that happen
so I called a passer-by

> We got him to The
> Samaritans
> and there I said
> Goodbye.
>
> A letter came to me one
> Day

A K Guest

IT COULD BE YOU

I'm huddled in a doorway, wrapped in a plastic sheet
Staring from an unwashed face as hailstones bounce along the street
Without a second glance, some people pass me by
While others watch quite slyly from the corner of their eye
Some put a coin into my hand, they can see I'm sleeping rough
I try not to ask for money though the going is quite tough
I'm praying for the night to finish and to see the dawn
When the shops will start to open and maybe I can get warm
I lost my job then lost my house, a victim of market force
Then sure as night must follow day my wife and I divorce
And now I've lost my doctor just as an added bonus
It seems you can't be registered when you're poor and homeless
Sometimes I feel so lonely and in deep despair
And as I look around me, I wonder if people care
I can't give in, there must be hope, I must believe or I cannot cope
I think of one of the sayings my teacher said to me
'In life people have their stations' rather quaint don't you agree?
Last night I watched the Mayor's Rolls Royce silently gliding by
And I smiled and thought to myself
'There but for the grace of God, go I'

Bob Boyd

SAVE OUR CITY!

To save our city
from all the pollution
there has to be
some kind of solution.

So save the whales
In the ocean deep
to stop our world
from falling asleep

Scrap you cars,
pile them up in a heap,
Be rid of iron bars,
So our animals may freely leap

So spare a copper,
Here and there,
Then hopefully we can breathe
clean, fresh air.

Fiona Root (15)

FINDING ME

The world outside looks at me
and when it does, what does it see?
A wife, a mother,
a daughter, a lover?

The mirror shows my face to me,
I look right back and what do I see?
A few more lines to mark my age,
no more for me the fresh turned page.

I look inside myself and what do I find?
A depth of spirit within my mind,
of things to learn, only half discovered,
a deep and dark, mysterious cupboard.

I've reached the stage of time for me,
to look beyond what mirrors see.
To reach for that ethereal goal,
to find myself, to find my soul.

Tina Dix

WHISTLESTOP

Whistlestop was our boat
That we sailed upon the sea
We'd dream about the voyages
Made by you and me
We sailed upon the roughest seas
And braved the fiercest gales
Stored up all the memories
For when we told the tales
In years to come when we were old
Content and satisfied
Of all of our adventures
That we had as a child
Unto our own we'd spin the yarns
For married we would be
Forgetting not that old tin boat
That bonded you and me.

Margaret Rose

WATER TIME

Like water I glide -
as boats rock on the mooring tide.
Filling up a ravine
often the marker's time has been.
Buoys and anchors
chain hope and land lubber words.
The beach
In summer played on, with iced drinks
The glasses' chinks,
the cups of tea swimming over
fill up pools - then bays and oceans.
More water pours in spouts,
the fishy mermaid's lips pouts.
By the fountain,
little trickles, tiddle down, and make
ripples, big as half-a-crown.
The drops
of the dripping tap are only seconds:
plip plopping away building small reserves
and issues.
The crush of a giant wave
fills up time between
and takes us out to sea.

David Hazlett

Rain

Rain drops fall from on high
Clouds billow in a stormy sky.
Branches droop with weight of rain
Soil inundated once again

Grass sodden underfoot
Gutters filled with gritty soup
Rivers overflow in watery doubt.
Banks covered in muddy grout

No let up on such a day
As rain drops fall once again.

B L R Jones

Oppressed

I'm locked up in a prison cell,
Made by you for me,
You think it's safe to keep me here,
And throw away the key.
But do you ever think about,
What it is I feel inside
The violence that you show to me,
The hurt I try to hide.
I doubt you'll ever understand
But maybe if you tried,
You'd find there's so much more to me,
Than what's on the outside.

Rhieanon Miles (16)

A Change Of Scene

Living in these modern times
Is no joke for an old fogey like me
Who was brought up in the old days
When there was much less liberty.
As I was born in nineteen sixteen
'Twas war-time in Britain then,
So it was poverty and hardship
And families without men.
At the time when I was in my teens
If a girl got pregnant she was 'put away',
Often into a mental institution
She was labelled 'guilty' so she was made to pay.
There's been a sexual revolution.
Permissiveness is now the way.
Homosexuals have come 'out of the closet'!
Guys no longer hide the fact that they're Gay.
Only one-in every-four girls get married
Illegitimacy is a fact of life,
Couples have a *partner* or a *relationship*
Or call themselves . . . common-law husband and wife!
Although I find it hard to be so liberal
After all marriage was the norm in my day,
I deplore the way divorce is . . . so easy
But at least folk now live their own way.
Maybe I'm just a wee bit jealous of their freedom
We were reared far too strictly, you see,
So good luck to the young folk of this age
The last decade of the Twentieth Century!

Mary Anne Scott

DEAR DADDY

Restless memories of you, force my weak
mind back into yesterday.
Creating for you a deliberation of hatred,
that won't just go away.
Everlasting pain, tortures the child who
sadly dwells within.
Now indebted with the endless cost,
for I was not conceived by God's love,
but from Satan's evil sin.
Your unending brutality, drove my
mother to abandon me.
Still unknown, she's eternally lost without
a trace.
My memories maybe trapped, but my
heart has found absolution.
And now, no longer afraid, I despise you.
You alone, are the source of my silent
tears,
which have marred my once innocent
face.
Oh father, I will never forget you, nor I
will ever forgive you.
Like you have never exonerated me,
for being your little mistake.
Yet, unlike you, I am self-sacrificing, and
without your neglectful piloting,
I will alone find tenderness, warmth
and devotion.

D M Bancroft

NIGHT TERRORS

I sit, fidgeting, on the bus.
Impatient, willing it to move through the darkness.
What false comfort those orange globes offer.

I am not fooled.
I know what danger lurks without.
The violence man aches to visit on his fellow man.
Eyes glowing red when they catch the light, feral.

Why is this man sitting behind me breathing so raggedly?
I hope he does not get off at my stop.
Go away.

Alighting, girding my loins for the long walk home that in daylight takes mere minutes.
Legs pumping, heart racing, my breath thunderous in my ears.
Will I even hear an approach from behind me?
Panic.

Nearly there, time to attempt a jog.
Damn that weak ankle.
Trembling hands inserting the key in a lock that won't stay still.
Stop moving.

Home, safe, relief, relax.

. . . until the next time.

Christina Ledwith

Darkness

Darkness is a void
A space in time where we relax
And yet we fear darkness
Is it because we're afraid of the unknown
Or afraid of change
Is the light so inviting
After all conflicts start in the light

We are more sociable at night
More happy, more welcoming
Yet we fear darkness
With relaxation comes peace
But with relaxation also comes darkness.

Ryan Hooper

Time

The finger of time moves on
Losing track of what has gone
No time to look back, regret
Best to look on, plan, forget
The sad times, remember glad times
To dwell in the past is a futile task
Ourselves we should ask
What good does it do to brew
Over hurts and slights we knew
Find in our hearts to forgive
Our path we should truly live
For no-one knows how long
Our journey among the throng
A tiny speck are we of humanity
In this vast endless eternity.

Eileen Gerrish

MEMORIES OF AN IMMIGRANT - 'THE FOUR SEASONS'

England how I long to see those shores so very dear to me
Busy cities filled with people, country towns with church and steeple
Bluebell woods and pretty dells, seasons with distinctive smells
But most of all I miss the place where I was born and bred and raised
'Tis way up north and on the east, sometimes too cold for man or beast
The winter wind blows cold and strong, days are short, nights are long
Then when it gets too much to bear, snowflakes fall covering everywhere
In a blanket, soft, crisp and white, lighting up the dreary night
To see this sight at Xmas season's a thing to cherish beyond time and reason
Jan and Feb continue cold, affecting people young and old
They're all decked out in warm attire, hurrying home to bright warm fire
But soon the snow it melts away, leaving places wet and grey
March arrives with winds and gales whistling through the hills and dales
Then April's spring is in the air, the gentle season mild and fair
Buds on trees all set to bloom, a welcome sight to lift the gloom
The special smell this season brings is long remembered with other things
Like warmer days and lighter nights, people now are feeling bright
Mams and grans all set to buy those gorgeous Easter eggs, oh my!
Cadbury, Thornton, Rowntree, Fry. Good old names that never die
Then comes May, the trees so green, lots of flowers to be seen
June, July and August brings thoughts of holidays and flings
Packing cases, feeling great, off to somewhere new old mate
Long warm summer days are here filling everyone with cheer
Schools are closed, children play, a time of rest you hear them say
September and October too conjure memories anew
Of autumn leaves all red and gold, weather now is turning cold
That nip is in the air again, another season on the twain

November with her wintry spells, then back to Xmas trees and bells
This place I miss is Geordieland, people there are really grand
Kind and thoughtful, down to earth, sense of humour cause for mirth
Times have changed we can't deny, but memories will never die.

Gloria Aldred Knighting

THE GARDEN

Our garden grows so many plants
With many varied hues
A peaceful place of beauty
With interesting views.

Where daffodils and tulips
Presented their spring show
Roses and geraniums
And the perennials grow.

The periwinkle trails its wreath
Upon the rustic bower
The clematis has reached beneath
Abundant with its flower.

These lovely flowers of summer will surely soon give way
To dahlias and begonias and humble marigold
Sweet William and chrysanthemum
In shades of brown and gold.

Then Christmas time arrives prepared with ilex tree
And is that mistletoe, I spy up in the apple tree?
The garden will reward your hours of energy
An annual collection of fragrant memory.

C Briggs

ONLY A NUMBER

Take-over bid . . . new company owner
Much renovation needed as workers commence
Adapting their skills well beyond their duties
Working all hours that God ever sent
New masters' promise their efforts rewarded
Assuring hard work will be *sweat* well spent
But on completion, the worker's forgotten
Company coffers fill with new profits at length
Misfortune befalls companyholic worker
Illness takes toll, for many months on end
How very soon he's forgotten by the masters
No phone call or card as to how he will mend
Statuary sick pay . . . is reward for *his* efforts
Fifty-two pounds . . . a few paltry pence
Considering his skills he used in his efforts
Thus saving the company considerable expense
Is it now any wonder, what our youth have to say
And *thumb their noses* at *loyalty*
To the *employers* of today
From personal experience, is it any wonder
When the employers of today, *treat you as a number*

Elizabeth A Hutchison

LOVE

Love is a gift
to all mankind
graciously sent from above
love gives itself
in humble trust
rests at peace in the heart
like a dove.

Like a gentle rain
it tenderly
waters the earth below
and the lowly take it
with delight
nurture and watch it grow.

E Smith

ICE MAIDEN

Dressed in delicate frost,
Of an icy blue,
A beauty so untouched,
Walks the earth,
In a cloud of cool mist,
She has a heart,
Made from purest snow,
She looks angelic,
With skin so pale of hue,
Her hair filled,
With silver shadows,
Her lips of,
The coolest arctic blue,
Her eyes,
They could bewitch you,
A mystery,
Veils her as a velvet blanket,
Her beauty,
Sets men's pulses racing,
But they,
Could never melt her heart.

Stacey Davis

REFLECTIONS

Reflections in the mirror,
Of one you used to know.
Reflections in the water,
Of one, I once, loved so.

Reflections of my life,
Of who I used to be,
Sat here, reminiscing,
Was that really me?

Reflections of the years,
As they've passed me by,
Reflections in my tears,
Every time I cry.

Reflections of my life,
And wondering where it went,
I think about the very, many,
Lonely hours I spent.

Why can't I be normal,
Like everybody else,
Why am I so different,
Just left upon the shelf.

Come and look into my heart,
I'm sure that you will see,
The person you've been searching for,
Could possibly be . . . me:

Deana Houghton

Dear Mum

From my childhood chrysalis
I emerge
Philandering limbs and emotions
Converge
My pillar of strength I implore
your help and your guidance
once more
When I dither on defiance
and scream accusations
restore our alliance
With your infinite patience
don't cripple my energy
Understanding bestow
grant redemption for my ignorance
Constrain me and know
a mere forced submission
is true humiliation
and flippant indignation
will perish my soul
don't exile but exalt
in my floundering ways
tentatively watch over me
all of my days
and when I endeavour
irreversibly wise
in voluptuous error
bring tears to your eyes
forgive me.

Finola Crudden

A Miner's Tale

Slowly we trudged down the road,
Breathing in the picturesque scene
Of dark satanic hills of coal slag;
In the background of the great winding wheel at the pit head
Slowly turning round; and screeching
As it lowers each cage,
Down into the bowels of the earth.

Looking at each face one by one
And remembering that they were only young men
Now aged; with coal in-grained skins
Looking old before their time
And have left their youth behind,
Down in the bowels of the earth.

As we are lowered down into the pit
Each of us send up a silent prayer
Hoping we'd see our loved ones again,
With our love we gave to them
In the darkness, we laboured
Down in the bowels of the earth.

How we laboured; Oh! What a sin
What we gave; and sacrificed
For our families we did strive,
Down in the bowels of the earth.

The day of the disaster,
There was a deathly rumble
As the pit collapsed,
The screaming of men could be heard
Echoing up the mine-shaft,
The nightmare had began
Down in the bowels of the earth.

As the rescuers descended,
Oh! What a tragedy,
Some were trapped, and some were dying,
And the sound of grown men crying.
Down in the bowels of the earth.

Up above the sirens were wailing,
The villagers knew, there had been a disaster,
The women were sobbing; wringing their hands in anguish,
Gradually the winding wheel took the cages to the surface,
And the smell of death was apparent.
Down in the bowels of the earth.

Now I lay dying; my end is near,
Gone are the memories of yesteryear,
The angel of death, is very near,
But, I will have no fear,
Down in the bowels of the earth.

Muriel M McLeod

NO RESTRICTIONS

Please don't try to tell me,
That you're too old for me.
For love has no restrictions,
On the age you have to be.
For time is passing quickly,
And soon it will be gone.
Time for regret,
Over things we should have done,
We shouldn't have to worry,
What other people say.
For the love and joy you bring me,
Can never be erased.

V Fazacherley

I Care Just As You

Ban the hand gun so you figure
It's not the gun, but who pull the trigger
So easy to point and say who's to blame
You're the one that blackens my name

My gun is for sport, for targets not people
A scapegoat I feel, I'll be a church with no steeple
You take my gun, but I've done no wrong
Why is it me that you're picking upon.

A gun is only as bad as one
That betrays the trust and a bad deed is done
My gun is secure, my ammo is too
So don't blacken my name, I care just as you.

Mike Lakey

I Wonder

Is life too short to look at you and smile,
Is there enough hours in a day to care a while,
Do our friends depend on what we can give,
Does our heart stop beating if we love to live,

We strive for peace, we'll strive forever,
A problem is halved if shared together,
Our deepest sadness subsides for now,
If we cry and laugh at least know how.

I wonder will love survive the test,
Will crime and hurt outgrow the test,
Will poverty, starvation always remain,
Will caring and kindness overcome the pain.

I wonder

Patricia Andrews

SEASHORE

I walked on the beach today.
        Saw fishermen in their yachts.
Children enjoying sand play,
        Including tiny tots.
The seagulls hovering high above.
        Against a clear blue sky
Searching frantically for tasty shells
        With luck they might espy
Eventually they make the choice,
        Swoop to take their pick
Unfortunately the shell is shut,
        So have to use the trick
They lift the shell in their beak,
        And fly very high
With a dash, the shell is dropped.
        To open as a pie,
Down come the seagulls
        Ready for a feed
No luck this time I heard one sigh
I'll take the shell up again,
        And have another try.
The second time meets
        With great success
Plonk the shell lands open wide
But the laughing seagull was fooled
There was nothing inside.

Win Dukelow

Fear

I am hurting deep inside,
This awful secret I must hide.
Is it fair what you have done to me,
Who can I tell please set me free.

I'm afraid I will lose my friends,
If I tell what happened then.
I was just a girl of eight,
When the abuse started I'm filled with hate,
I feel so dirty deep inside,
My thoughts are spinning where can I hide.

People they all look at me,
I feel so guilty can they see.
Don't you know it's not my fault,
I screamed and cried and begged let go.
But I was just a child you see,
He wouldn't stop and set me free.

Jean Hollings Grant Ross

Dreams

Dreams can be magic,
Dreams can cause pain,
Pictures in living colour,
Flashing through your brain.

Real life drama,
When you are asleep,
Dreams can be simple,
Dreams can be deep.

Dreams that can frighten,
Dreams that make no sense,
Dreams that can calm one,
When you go to bed all tense.

Dreams can be happy,
Dreams can be sad,
But if it wasn't for our dreams,
We'd all be raving mad.

Larry Bowen

THE LADY OF THE LAKE

When the early morning's whispers
Ruffle my curtains, I identify you
Untainted and opaque;
The autobiography of a matchless dimension
On which I labour to live . . .

So stirring in purity, recherché
On the material level, you gleam
Through the water in a soporific smile.
An intimation of the Garden of Eden,
How the essence was meant to be.

Swan, do not refrain from reaching;
Do not waver on the waves
Or turn from the current's ardent arms
We are artfully adjoined here,
Yet will soon be universally united . . .

Michele Glazer

UNTITLED

Once, things seemed different,
Now all things seem the same.
The way they were in the past, stop,
it's all going too fast. Lord, you have cast me a rotten deal.

Little things, like merciful doves, bewilder us, to all of those,
Who have had a response to those countless loves.

Many, tiny, small beings,
have very big, huge feelings,
Things which follow us, and go out of our mind,
Things which come back, and make us feel left behind.

The things we are given in our time
Means we should express gratefulness, not selfishness

Tracey Rush

BEEN LONELY

Being lonely is a funny feeling in a way
You feel unwanted by people day by day
If you try and think, sad things just come out
These thoughts make you want to scream and shout
But nothing comes out except drops of tears
Memories and thoughts from years and years
By that point you feel like you want to die
But you don't really know the reason why
All you need is someone to hold you tight
And tell you everything will be all right
Not someone to ask questions and shout at you
Just someone to understand the way you're feeling too
When this person comes and brings no pain
You'll be happy and never lonely again.

Janine Dickinson

Resolution Of An Artist

Acceptance of what is possible;
Makes it doubly easier to choose.
Resistance to the reality of circumstances;
Bites into the mind of creativity.

Coming to terms with practicalities;
Opens the flood-gates;
Into the realms of possibilities;
'Grasping the Nettle', presents challenge.

Self-knowledge of one's limitations;
Makes practicalities surmountable.
Danger lurks with illusions of grandeur;
Wherein self-deception lies.

An abundance of 'common' sense;
Makes options feasible.
Knowledge of what is available;
Widens the scope of limitations.

Limitations can vary from none to infinity;
Making the options available limitless.
'Cutting your Cloth', accordingly;
Creates security of control.

Putting knowledge into practice;
Is putting the horse before the cart.
Making the possibilities endless;
And extremely fascinating to the artist, who creates.

Alastair Buchanan

Little Blue Bear

There's a little blue bear
Who sits on the shelf
She looks lonely there all by herself
She cannot see, she cannot talk
She was yours even before you could walk
She holds so many memories dear
Of your cuddling her close in those early years
She saw your laughter
She's seen your pain
Since you've been gone, for no-one's life's been the same,
Your little blue bear holds pride of place
Every time I look at her, I see your smiling face
Your little blue bear holds memories dear
Memories I hold forever near.

Ka Lunnon

Together Again

Lightning struck
At the moment we kissed
Our thoughts were so full
Of the things we had missed
Our hearts were so frail
Our hands held so strong
Our lost time apart
Was far too long
The sky clapped with thunder
So heavy the rain
Once more we kissed
Together again.

Melvyn Roiter

Remember Me

Do not weep
I am not dead,
I am the stars
Above your head.

I am the lips
That kiss your face,
And the strong arm that holds you
In a warm embrace.

I am the wind
That blows in the trees,
And the beautiful flower
That bends in the breeze.

I am the dark shadow
In your room at night
Keeping watch
Till the morning light.

I am the wave
That kisses the shore
Remember me
I am no more.

Joan Rastall

NOCTURNE

I look towards the sky
And see a high
Lone star
Cradled in a broken cloud
(The day's shroud
Crumbling into night)
Its pallid light
Pale as your slender arms.

Do you see it, too, I wonder,
Through your darkling window, yonder?
Do you hear the words
I urge it to convey
Before the day
Draws down the blinds?

Be still - be still -
And you will hear it call your name,
Will hear the quiet beating of a heart
That, though apart from you,
Is yet a part of you.

Be still - be still -
Stiller than a painted moon -
And you will hear the
Lone star
Whisper in your ear -
'I love you'.

John Davies

THE RETURN OF THE SWALLOW

Replenish the dusk
repertoires at night's door
endearing exhibitionists
you've returned to our shore
your unfathomable journey
of self-preservation
has a valuable lesson
to teach to this nation
your hedonistic host
all knowing mankind
whose misconstrued energies
are terminally primed
needs reminding that seasons
and sunsets and swallows
will continue to exist
no matter what follows
rapturous rivers will continue to flow
meticulously cleansing mother nature's abode
immortality is disturbingly reserved for the soul
but mankind focused firmly on attaining this goal
forgot about living and lavishing in life's mystery
inherited scepticism sliced crevasses in history
while we continue to transmute turmoil and torture
the swallow will exist
on the wings of nature and nurture.

Finola Crudden

THE INDUSTRIAL WASTE

Just when you thought it was coming to an end,
The blood spewed out of your mouth, the pain returned again,
The factories glistened in the dark, and all was cold,
The churning of the machines vibrate into the soul.

The children darted underneath the factories they hate,
Rolling in the dust and dirt, the excrement and waste,
Some of them with little faces, cuts and ravaged sores,
Crying out for the end to come, but the industry wanted more.

The man made the money, the children kept the pain,
He needed more workers, for him they would be slaves,
There was nothing but pure hatred, left within his mind,
He was completely numb now, greed is all you'll find.

The sun it shone no more, the children's eyes were black,
Their clothes torn and tattered, bloody lesions on their backs,
The man he wanted more, the children had to be lean,
For they were the workers of the industrial machine.

He fed off their suffering, and relished in their pain,
The clouds began to burst, the man he was insane,
The blood rubbed on their faces, they kept the wheel alive,
Churning out the rubbish, dirt rubbed in their eyes.

The deafening screams and tortured moans of the ones he raped,
Their torn flesh and bleeding, the pain that he creates,
To quench his domination, the children had to die,
The factory stood there desolate, without them it could not survive,
The man stood amongst the corpses, his final and last mistake,
He'd destroyed his money in the industrial waste.

The children's silent voices cry out in vain,
He punished them with fire, burning flesh is what he craved,
The man stood their laughing, his domination had been cursed,
Ashes spilled from the sky and the ground began to burst.

Angela Speyers

OUR VALLEY'S BUS ROUTE TO ROMANCE

I see your bus go fleeting by,
You smile my way, I want to cry.
But then I hear the brakes applied,
And my poor heart just bursts with pride.
For here, at last, you've noticed me,
I've waited here since half-past three!
For someone said you always stop
For twenty minutes by this shop.
If I'm in luck, they said, you might
Lock up the bus, as you alight.
Then wander over to my flat,
And knock my knocker - rat, tat, tat.
I shout to you from where I stand,
I'm over here, please take my hand.
Yes I am Betty, I sent the note;
You've come to see me and report!
Your name is Colin I've been told,
You see that I am freezing cold.
You hold my hands and make them hot,
You give a wink and that's my lot.
I take you over to my flat,
We go inside, I take your hat,
I hang your jacket on the hook,
Then we embrace. You give that look,
That look that says 'Yes you're for me,'
My eyes respond, how I agree!
And now forever you are mine,
Oh yes, my darling Valentine.

Charles Ivor Morris

LOVE IS

Love is what you make it, no sorry a misquote.
Life is what you make it, yes, I should have remembered,
After all that has happened these past years,
I was not born a cynic, I was not born a masochist,
Yet these two characteristics seem to have developed without
                                              being invited.

Love is beautiful, all too consuming, it takes over your very soul,
As I remember, and oh that feeling of impatience as you wait to
                                                see him again.
The passion that takes over as he holds you all through the night,
The closeness, the abandonment of any inhibitions that you may
                                                have once had.
True love has this effect, it captivates your mind and body,
                                                it is all powerful;
You live from moment to moment, you hang on his every word,
                                                even on the telephone,

And when he doesn't ring you become manic,
Then he does ring and you feel so high you could have taken a
                                                bottle of valium.
The joy of love is so intense, three little words mean everything,
You hang on to them, smile inside as you recall, the time he
                                                first spoke them;

Magical times, dream times, cherish them, remember them always.
Sadly, things and people change, the love you once thought you had,
May become less loving, forget to tell you he cares,
Probably, because he has yielded to another temptation,
He doesn't know how to tell you, cannot hurt you, but is doing so,
                                                because of it.

You die a little each day. You see him less, the phone calls
                                                become more infrequent,
He makes excuses, pressure of work, stress! That wonderful,
                                                oh so useful word,
You try to believe him, but as the months pass, you know he has
                                                lied and is lying still.
A broken heart holds together by a thread;
You try to walk tall, but you stumble so many times,
As you remember his face, demeanour, voice, once so loving,
                                                now that of a stranger's.
Time passes, it gets no better, how does one fall out of love, when
                                                so in love with perfection.
You try to remove the rose coloured spectacles, but you still see
                                                him as he was.
Your amour, your God; suffice to say, things will not change, he
                                                has moved on,
It is only *you,* who have not, still loving, still hurting . . .

Amanda-Lea Manning

UNWANTED GIFT

Please give me back my heart,
It isn't yours to keep.
And you tricked me into loving you,
Then you stole it piece by piece.
Send back all my kisses,
That I gave you wrapped in love.
And please don't forget my sweet embrace
That fit you like a glove.
And so you don't forget me
Throughout the passing years.
I've wrapped a present just for you
And sent you all my tears.

Sue Allison

TRAFFIC JAM

It's ten to nine, the line is never ending
I've had three warnings from the boss this week.
'If you don't pull your socks up Mr Simon Peeweek
You'll be down at the dole office
Collecting your week's keep and that
Isn't much you'll be losing some sleep'

The horns are blowing, the tension's growing
The boss isn't knowing
I'm in this jam.

But all is mistaken
He is only making is way to the
office on my left hand side.

'Good morning,' he says
'I'll give you extra pay if you don't
mention you saw me on this very day'
'Certainly not sir' I said in good humour.
It pays to be late of ten better than not.

Rosline Allen Gayle

A BEGINNING

Your helpless face looks up at me,
you search for things you cannot see.
This different place, from where so warm?
An amazing day that you were born.

Your tiny hands and short, pink feet,
your perfect form, so small, so neat.
Your skin as soft as pure white snow.
A dream like day, only mothers can know.

When a day in a life has just begun,
it will stay forever, like a song that's been sung.
This tiny being that means so much,
I will love and cherish with every touch.

A Carrigan

PATHETIC PARENT

Sobbing profoundly at the ineptitude of parenthood
Then gazing catatonically into the darkness
Plunging ever further towards a manic mood
Standing scarred in naked starkness.

Unblissfully aware of dishonour, no stranger to disgrace
Sinking further into introverted solitude with a stoic face
A failing parent, a broken man
Sunk into the depths of unfathomable space.

A fragmented heart adding torment and torture to frustrated impotency
Wincing wistfully at the pain
Wishing one could try again
Wailing woefully once more, pleading for clemency.

The Muses aware of the agony
Bow their heads and turn away
Where does one get justice?
And what more can one say?
Your son, that minor miracle
The one you love far more than gold
The one that in your ineptitude
You've forgotten how to hold.

Timothy Alexander

SOMETIMES

Sometimes I hasten to add
That I'm glad of the semantic, or attitude.
What comes, with it is, gratitude,
Which leaves nothing, like lassitude.

It's complacency, and practicality,
Which leads to frutality,
It doesn't, bring unity,
or calamity.

It's pure true, happiness,
gentle, and kind, and youthful,
nothing like the things,
that are not political.

It's in groups which are collective
and very selective,
It isn't prolific,
It's simplistic.

The love of God,
Is direct, and outstanding,
It's pure,
and understanding.

To go on your way,
and believe, then you,
will realise, that you,
never can be deceived.

C McAloon

INSTINCTS

Believe in your instincts they're usually correct
in your heart you can almost detect
Especially when your health is low
with a peace you've not long to go
A strange feeling to keep to yourself
a part of life I have plenty of wealth

Wealth in love as some never know
heartache, pain, all part of the show
Friends in abundance, such a precious gift
children, laughter life passes so swift
I was a child it seems forever
grow up grow older, some never

We all of us die when the time is right
it's strange to think there's nothing to fight
When you know someone is waiting for you
to accept the inevitable that's for true
Born into life expect the best
go out alone eternal rest

There's nothing sad about living dying
we're here to learn no cheating lying
Beauty in almost all you will find
the good the bad is all in the mind
Learn from your pain, give to others
what you have gained being a mother

So privileged to be part of a minute particle
in a small way contribute with an article
On life on love as you see it today
perhaps tomorrow it will all slip away
Pain is such an individual thing
to tell the truth I want to sing . . .

Jean Tennent Mitchell

LOSING YOU

For a lifetime it seems
You haunted my dreams
A little more each day,
I loved you
A little more each day,
I wanted you
A little more in every way,
Now I look into your eyes
And I'm quick to realise
I'm losing you -
A little more each day;
I'd be a fool to pretend
I know this is the end,
So, what else can I do -
But wish the pair of you
Happiness - a little more each day.

Thomas C Ryemarsh

SKETCHES

Today is the day to be happy.
Tomorrow may be too late.
Only the present is certain,
Foolish are those who would wait.

Make use of the blessings God gave you,
Or else He will take them away.
Remember things fade rather quickly,
Enjoy all your gifts while you may.

Happiness stays but a moment,
But very few realise this.
Seldom can people recapture,
A moment of heavenly bliss.

So it is I who sends this message,
To all who tread life's toilsome road.
Live every day to the fullest.
It may be the last episode.

William Price

A SCHOOL

School starts in the morning.
Lessons can be boring
Teachers arriving late, pupils even later
Breaktimes are fun to have an interesting conversation
The canteen has several sticky iced buns
Bells that are so loud are to keep the time
Assemblies have many notices
In the lunch hour there are enjoyable clubs
There is basketball, maths and art clubs
School trips are fascinating
Homework is often given
Uniforms are worn, with a liking
Sometimes the fire-bell goes off
Always causing nervousness
Exams are taken every year
Most pupils try to do the best they can
A prize is awarded for the best student
Sports day are full of energetic runners
Lessons end in the afternoon
Pupils leave the building, then it is cleaned.

Basma Tafsirullah

MOMENTS

Fierce in defence
Of its territory
Perched on a branch
In the Forest of Dean
A robin redbreast
Carols above
With a rapturous, savage
Sweet song of love . . .

And oh!
I remember in long years of leisure
Those few stolen moments
Of idyllic pleasure
Snatched from the routine
Of mundane affairs
As we stood in the
Frost spangled madrigal air . . .

Lovers ensnared
Momentarily
Neath a beautiful
Sunlit canopy . . .

By a rapturous, savage
Sweet song of love . . .

Delia Marheinshe

REBIRTH

Elfin seraph caught in moonbeam
Sways in time with will 'o' wisp,
Glides, sways, as of a dream -
Serenades softly, sweetly, crisp -
An overture to glory.

Swooping from their silent 'eyries'
Crane and heron circle, red
Hot orbs darting queries,
Crackling questions left unsaid,
Challenges from time hoary.

Then falcon bursts upon the scene -
Vile viper lurks to measure
Lethal strike, cold and clean,
Demean that which we'd treasure;
Sly entrant by back door, he.

But graceful stalks this lord of sky,
Knowing well such darker craft -
Shuns wicked kiss, and bite:
Victorious, he revelled, laughed
'Midst ovation to glory . . .

. . . of Michael's dream reborn.

Phoenix J Martin

BLEATING

I cried wolf all day,
And finally you were one.
Our long-awaited life,
I spread before us,
Scintillating!
Like sharp and glinting shards,
To trap our feet and lame us.
Living on dreams -
That could not really feed us.
The hope like a tightrope
To stretch out between our sorrows.
How I must have hurt you!
That I could not call a spade a spade,
You turned your hardened hands
Up to the sky; asking me,
Straight out: 'Believe in me!'
And I could not
And I could not hold fast to life.
Your words, like temporary birds,
They circle, and pass over
Without ever really meaning.
Now you are gone from me,
Finally.
The wolf I made of you, playing to my lamb,
The lamb is now a sheep of course.
Still bleating away.

Tess Bates

HARMONY

The flowers - the trees
Whisper in the breeze;
Dew running off
To water the moss.

Bees and butterflies
Dancing above,
With wings so fine
Transparent to the eye.

Birds singing
Not far away,
Calling out
Night is on its way.

The moon - the stars
A romantic night,
Everything beautiful
In our sight.

Warm night air
As we sit and stare.
Cuddled close in a warm embrace
Your gentle lips - kissing my face.

Whispering words
Of love devine,
You surrendering
Your magic charm.

Trees nearby - rustle their leaves
Making music in the breeze.
Snuggled close - close as can be
Here we are in harmony.

Margaret J Franklin

THE 30S CROWD ON SATURDAY NIGHT

The 30s crowd were leaner, rougher,
Thronging the streets on Saturday night.
Skirts were longer, shoes were tougher,
Bought to last, for money was tight.

A happy, bustling, shouting mob,
Spilling forward, down the steps
Been to watch the latest heart throb,
Now the cry is 'Fish and chips!'

Market stalls with flare lights spluttering
Lighting up the tasty wares,
Dance-hall gay with banners flutt'ring
'Come on in, forget your cares.'

Friend meets friend in local boozer,
No TV screen to keep them in.
'No wireless yet? Well, you're the loser,
Come along and have a gin.'

The speech they used was different too,
All the same for youth and age,
No discotheque, and lav for loo,
Youthful pranks, not senseless rage.

Girl and boy went to the pictures,
She with tight crimped wavy hair,
Securely held, with grips as fixtures,
Hand in hand their joy to share.

They might have seen the youthful Gable
Laughed together at Mickey Mouse
Then GB news with fact not fable,
Before the organ shook the house.

Their weekly glimpse of heaven ended,
And the National Anthem played
In gloomy streets their footsteps wended,
And their future plans were laid.

The boys all tried to look their best,
Hair sleeked back with brilliantine,
Short back and sides, not like a nest.
Hair on shoulders never seen.

People hanging round the meat stalls,
'Have they much to give away?'
Further on a swaying man falls,
'Too much to drink' the people say.

Staggering on with friends beside him,
Mouth a'slobber, retching, sick,
Pushed into his open landing,
Falls against the grey, bare brick.

The market stalls are empty now
The strangled shouts soon die away
The copper mops his sweaty brow
And midnight starts another day.

Celia Turner

TEARS

Tears are cried for so many reasons
Tears are cried for births
Tears are cried for deaths
Tears are cried for pain
Tears are cried for joy
Tears are cried for sadness
Tears are cried for happiness
Tears are cried for so many reasons
And for many more to come.

Maria Tangen

To Stress

O bane of my life how persistent you are!
You are with me night and day
You follow me where'er I go
You are everywhere!

I go to work and you are there
Crouched like an animal ready to pounce
Anxiety and pressure means you are doing your job
You are everywhere!

Home I go and to bed I turn
For solace rest and peace
You interfere with my night's sleep
Yes you are everywhere!

But I must not let you get me down
It's important to show you that I'm the boss
You may have a purpose but I must cope
Because you are everywhere!

If you went away I'd feel the loss
You are the stimulus that causes adrenaline to flow
Because of you jobs are well done
And you are everywhere!

Anne Mackle

The Swallow

On the wing swiftly flies the swallow
Darting thither and thither,
Zooming through the air like a bullet
Coming fast as the night draws to a close
At last now each sleeps as through thick branches they follow,
Parting thither and thither.

Likewise in their soft leafy beds,
No sound is heard from their gracious heads
Corrupt and conquer is their basic skill
But in their hearts none can tell for all is still
Though in sweet air flies the swallow,
Baring no waiting, just follow,
Darting, parting, thither and thither.

Christine Conway

NATURE'S GIFTS

As the mist enshrouds the mountain tops,
You're alone upon the hills.
A sense of peace surrounds you,
Yet your heart and mind it thrills.

The whistle of the soft light wind,
So cool but fresh and sharp.
The greeting of the skylark's call,
So sweet yet like a harp.

The rustling murmur, of the trees,
The curlew's chilling call.
The pitter patter, of the rain,
The clattering waterfall.

So peaceful, yet rewarding,
To the eye and ear, delight.
The view before you, ever new,
With the changing of the light.

'It's there, for all who seek it,
You can wander there at will.
'It's nature's gift, to everyone,
All there, so take your fill.

E M Dolphin

The Last Rose Of Summer

In the feeble blush of morning sun
The autumn air hangs cold and chill
Yet there resplendent on a bush
A single rose it lingers still.

Drenched deep in ghostly morning mist
Each petal laced with crystal dew
All other blossoms long since shed
Companions that it never knew.

Its perfumed fragrance beckons all
Its unique beauty few will view
A vestige of a summer past?
Or a token for a summer new?

Michael Creed

Come Back

I love you how could you do this to me
You left me alone crying for love
Like the wind blowing over the ocean you flew into my heart
But like a bird you could not stay you are a free spirit
You spread your wings and went away
I need you my love
I need to feel your strong arms around my body
I need to hear your voice to feel your breath upon my face
My love for you will always be like the ocean never ending
The waves are like drums beating against my heart
Oh how I wish to see your face just once more
For our eyes to meet
For you to gaze upon my face
Come back to me my love, come back.

Lyn Cabble

WHEN LIAM MET LENNON

Mad for it music is the basis
Of the band they call Oasis;
But before the ascent of the Gallagher brothers
The formula belonged to four fab others
George, Ringo, John and Paul -
Some might say they invented it all
And if the tunes and tantrums sound familiar
Wait till they auction the memorabilia . . .

The Beatles split up when Oasis were babies
But the sounds stay around - Definitely Maybe
Did John see visions through meditation
Of Liam signing to Creation?
Oasis got into legal tussles
Ripping off the Fab Four and the Ruttles,
But Tomorrow Never Knows, it could have been worse -
Imagine the Beatles sung by the Smurfs!

John married Yoko, they had Instant Karma
Liam's got Patsy for Gucci glamour
Throughout the media their stories unfurled
A circular vision of the world
Lennon McCartney, Liam and Noel
What's The Story? Rubber Soul
From Manchester City to Menlove Ave
Don't Look Back in Anger, All You Need is Love.

Angela White

THE POET'S SONG

They travel worlds and centuries long,
The poets rhyming rhythmic songs.
Dancing through the shades of life,
Capturing laughter love and strife.
They speak of birth and all mankind,
Or liken age; to summer wine.

Words spin like endless webs of gold,
Enfolding senses and the soul,
Weaving dreams to steal the mind,
which gently floats away in time;
Seeing mellow days take flight,
To purple shadows of the night.

Like trusted friends the poems stay,
And walk beside you on life's way.
Sighing softly on the wind,
To say. The song will never end!
As poets hear the whispering world;
And write their rhythmic spoken words.

D M Gale

NOW I WALK WITH HIM

He walked with me in the sunlight,
  He walked with me, in the rain.
He made me feel so happy.
  But he also shared my pain.

He held my hand, in the moonlight,
  He held my hand, when I cried.
He made me feel alive again.
  When the heart inside me died.

He walked with me in the gardens.
  He listened so patiently.
He told me none of his troubles.
  His thoughts were just for me.

Now I walk with him. In the darkness,
  I gently take his hand.
And remember the days, he walked with me.
  Along the shifting sands.

Hazel P Marsay

FANTASY

To travel from wherever you want
To any place you'd like to go
Is part of a dream
Is part of a plan
No rain, no wind, no snow

To float around
In a fantastic way
With gossamer soles on your feet
A thin golden thread
Form an anchor so strong
Will make the picture complete

To bring from the clouds
To sing from your soul
Of fantasy bubbling on high
A rich golden key
Will bring a reward
And the gossamer thread will not die.

Mary Hulme

IN THE STILL OF THE NIGHT

It's the middle of the night and all around is still
Nothing to be heard, hardly a sound the air does fill

The distinguished hoot of an owl, or the rustle of the trees
Hearing barely nothing, just slight movement in the breeze
Each house mostly in darkness, an odd light here and there

Stillness lies across the land, people dreaming without a care
Twigs snap in the silence, an animal's feet lands on the ground
In the sky the bat flies, heading for a place to hang around
Lowering of the sunset, setting down in the dark skies
Lull before the new day starts and waiting for sunrise

Out in the yonder of darkened sky, stars sparkle and a moon shines
Fading slowly as the sun rises, fading into nothing, nowhere, no signs

The night is for nocturnals, to whom our night turns into their day
Hedges, holes, burrows and nests, is where they hide away
Each night is very different, some are warm, and some have frost

Not many people are about, a path rarely walked or bridge is crossed
In the dead of night an eerie silence, so quiet, you can hear a pin drop
Gone is the noise and the bustle of the day, at night it's at a stop
Hoots, howls, barks, and more as the wildlife language is in flow
Tomorrow as the sun comes up, it's a world that we never know.

Belinda Pyett

AFRICA'S BUSH

When the lion stalks his prey
The bush keeps still;
When the hippos go under water
Everything is startled,
When the zebra trots
All the stripes cover the bush.

When the spotted eagle flies
The song fills the air. The hyena laughs
The other animals flee
When the moon shines
Brighter than the stars.

Diandra Glazer (7)

GOOD-BYE

My world collapsed,
As I could not say
My last goodbye,
Her heart was strong
Her body was weak
With thoughts of her
There was no sleep;

The months were long
My heart would ache
Although she suffered
She never knew why
But near the end
Her eyes would not lie
So when she had taken
Her heavenly place

I kissed goodbye
On my mother's face;
With my heart feeling pain
And feeling alone
The room was so silent
The goodbye was long.

Ann Maurie

SIGNS OF SPRING

The sun strokes colour into blades of grass,
The dew drops glisten like pieces of cut glass,
The creatures stir in their camouflaged beds
and young green shoots raise their flowery heads.

Rippling water gently shimmers across the pond,
The surface is clear now the icy crust has gone,
Reeds join in the celebration dance of freedom
and fish scales flash beneath the rising sun.

The breeze whispers softly amongst the trees
and tender boughs display their new-born leaves,
Winter feathers moult with the fluttering of wings
and the birds let everyone know that it is spring.

Kathleen Speed

HEAD SAILOR

Prance in my tight leggings attire
For all to see aboard thy ship at sea
To survey the sights that would make me feel
like such a gentleman while on my ship at sea
To my crew I take the view I would ask no more
For to work pull thy anchor inset sails
My sailors mop thy deck tarry for the whip
You'll feel make haste sing as you work
Make haste never tarry for I'll be
like the sea to thee.

K Latham Grimes

LETTING GO

The light went out when you died.
The moon ceased to shine, the stars lost their glitter,
I felt sad, bereft, undone,
And just a shade bitter.
Why me? I asked, as I picked up the pieces
With sympathy from daughter, sons, nephews and nieces.
It helped a little, to hear their commendation
What a brave soul he was, having fought for the nation.
Worked hard for charities, selfless, no thought for self
Always the underdog,
His requirements on the shelf.

He was old, a world of experience behind him.
Trying to gain knowledge, always querying you'd find him.
So he was gone.
I accepted the fact
And gave thought to, the womb, the foetus, that a mother sought to
Treasure, cherish and nurture, something it ought to.
Sadly the seed in time didn't develop
With heartbreak that mother in grief to envelop.
A child at a crossing, a car, lights ignoring
It happens so often, the death rate still soaring.

A man in his twenties
With all life before him
This is until the good specialist saw him.
Cut down in his prime, all his laughter is finished.
The hopes of his loved ones so sadly diminished.
My loved one gone and a wealth of regretting,
No tears any more, no heartache or forgetting.
Three score years and ten, why he laughed at that number.
He reached eighty seven, so why not let him slumber?

Doris Holland

Rainbow

What is over the rainbow?
People say pots of gold,
We'll never know.

Does it last forever?
Do the clouds float with it
Will it ever end?

Has God got it tied up in his heart?
Is there another world over there where pixies play?
Is it full of endless dreams where fairies sing lullabies?

Is it another heaven where good people go?
Will people ever know what goes on in this wonderland?
I wonder,

It slowly starts to fade away,
Will it ever come back?
The sky goes back to normal sad and glum.

Kate Douglas (14)

Ebb And Flow

Gannets down the edge tide
Bathers now are gone
Salty waves are dashing
On to pier and prom.

Snaking into fissures
Ebony the slabs
Slavered white and lunar
Hides the bubbling crabs.

Western skies now flaming
Cauterise the rim
Molten rock pools silent
Captures all within.

Calder of the ocean
In undulating might
Below the inky canopy
Roam tidal soft tonight.

Clive W Macdonald

TRUE LOVE

We fell in love a long time ago,
Though you may not remember.
I loved you so,
Maybe we were too young to realise our state,
By then we had parted,
And our love was too late,
You went your way and left me behind,
But after all these years I still find,
You still have the power to make me smile,
To hold your hand,
And pause for a while,
Why was our love denied us both,
We could not understand,
So we must go forth,
Taking through life what might have been,
The yearning and hoping were all unforeseen,
You'll always be with me wherever I go,
Through all that has happened,
I still love you so.

Win Davies

THE PRISONER

She had a parlour - it possessed her
Private perfect and polished
A tomb of rich lavender wax

Sacred, sparkling glass cabinet
Trophies of bone, china tea cups
Washed weekly used rarely
Waiting for a funeral

Footstep free carpet
Carefully placed cushions
On wrinkle free sofa

Still white lace curtains
Washed weekly
Peeped through often

Posh parlour grate
And Wedgewood ornaments
Dusted daily
Gazed at often

Soot free chimney
Swept often used never
Shiny brass companion set
Never glinting in the warmth of a fire

She stares in horror
Old bed placed in the midst of her perfection
Commode nearby
Her prison now complete.

Stephanie Hulley

LOVE IS

Love is
An emotion deep inside,
A feeling or sensation
Hard to describe.
Love is
A smouldering fire,
Busting into flame
As passion transpires.
Love is
To have and hold,
Cuddling close
When nights are cold.
Love is
Unselfish, never unkind,
Grievances aired,
No axe to grind.
Love is
Sometimes pain,
A storm in a teacup,
Peace regained.
Love is the answer,
For living for life,
For man and woman,
For trouble and strife.

Polly Cox

INCLINE OF DAY

The light of today breaks tomorrow's darkness,
Pulling through the purple rain of perception,
without light there is no darkness,
All you see is the open wide space of desolation,
Where nothing knows why,
The chilled extinction of life leaving open mind,

I see the day the night the darkness follows,
But with one glance it dies,
Feeding on energy it grows till day,
One eye lies on us and the other on what will happen next,
As he controls the script on what one man will do on all
                                        our tomorrows,
The third eye lies upon our future,
Far away even further than our children's,
Children's birth,
A tear falls

It can't be seen,
But it still lies upon,
Like the wind you feel the effects,
It can be seen by one,
the chosen one,
the man of exotic measures of mankind,
the breeder of goodness and life,
whom lies above all,
the key to freedom,

The unstoppable feeling still lies upon evil,
but without evil whom would of thought of good,

        goodness lies upon and is the only door to the next day.

Lee Laidlaw

FRIEND

She stands alone,
Hair flowing free,
An accent her own,
A writer to see.

Determination,
In-depth feeling,
Stories to be told,
With a strength so bold.

A person of liking,
Innocent with charm,
Laughter about her,
Amazing and free.

A person likeable,
Protecting her children,
A love so pure,
Others can see.

A writer, a mother,
A friend to me.
Christina is all
A person should be.

Mary Jo West

THE CUCKOO

Full sun his emerald fire smart
  the greenhouse glass.
Grey cuckoo cock so oft repeat
  his name, give joy again,
It be a human call, cannot
  be bird at all.
The first time heard,
  still love the thieving bird.
Watch every tree, ne'er
  find the one he be.
Fed by April tear, his
  blossom here.
Mauve moistened glade,
  pale smocks delight the maid.
Dew silver drop the leaf,
  where Heaven's colours peep.
Sunrise, geranium, blazing,
  red, man still abed.
Warm pots astore the
  greenhouse floor.
Not one be lost, good angel
  banish frost.
Sun mote amingle cuckoo note,
  whilest bird in wood remote,
  sip egg into his throat.

A E Doney

IF OUR EYES COULD ONLY SPEAK

They fill the streets, the shops, the homes
and dance and shine with youthful charm.
I search for those that warmth must show,
that speak the words I long to hear.

From platforms high they look at me
or cast so low we fail to meet.
Some glance and near me steal
but silence is of no avail.

My pleading eyes beg them to stay,
my lips are tight, my heart thumps loud,
I cannot speak the words I know,
I pray to *God* to help me now
to find those eyes I long to see,
that they may closely speak with mine,
and stay within my heart.

D S Arthur

NO DIST...

...ns, our special day,
...your love for me across the
that divide us.
Your tender loving kisses are still on my
lips, and your love and kindness is all
around me.
Apart from having you here, what more could
I want, when your loving heart is within
me, and memories of bygone days entertain
me as consolation.

Donna Dudley

WEDDING BLUES

The young lady brushed her golden hair
and thought of the gown she had to wear.
For tomorrow was her wedding day,
Starting life a different way.
She thought, what would the future hold,
if the love they shared grew cold.
She must not doubt her future life
but become a loving and caring wife.

Do other brides fear their future so,
surely the love they have should grow
and continue on its blissful way
beyond their Golden Wedding Day.

Barbara Pickles

SUMMER'S DAY

Thru' tranquil woo—
Long country lanes with br—
My thoughts are focused, how I wish—
Was free of inner city strife.

Where splendid oak and sycamore
Cast umbrella shadows for cattle to go
To laze around after hours of graze
Escape midday sun in summer's haze.

Over butterfly meadows down to silver stream
Passing fields of poppies dancing it does seem.
The smells and sounds of the country on a
Summer's day.
Makes my life in the city seem miles away . . .

Patrick Humble

Weekend Away

Arriving at Windsor, the downpour abating,
The car pulls up then sighs with relief,
Above us the wire fingered branches are reaching,
To skies that are clearing and in whom we've belief.

Refreshment is needed, our repast is simple,
Some bread, some cheese, that suits us just fine,
Spread out there before us, a feast for the weary,
And to top it all off, a nice bottle of wine.

We stepped from the park and made moves to the river,
The grey swirling Thames moving effortlessly,
Upstream it meandered toward Henley and Oxford,
And downstream it glistened, gliding on to the sea.

To have you to myself, with no others demanding,
Is a treat rare to find in our bustling life,
No pressure, no hassle, no phone calls, no children,
Just you and I, my lover, my wife.

Above stands the castle, so proud and so solemn,
Its defences now broken with a simple nine quid,
Attacked almost daily, the massed swarms of tourists,
We didn't go in, but the 'Yanks' they sure did.

So off to our evening, an hotel near Langley,
Executive level, with enormous bed,
To while away hours of impassioned splendour,
To foreclose on hatred so our love may be fed.

Rob Baston

SILENCE

If silence were all around and no breath taken,
no laughter found. If night was eternal, and day never broke.
I will love you.
Never knowing tears or whispers from strangers.
Not seeing springtime or pictures of angels,
no holding hands, or tenderly touching fingertips.
Never pressing lips to lips,
I will love you.

B Baker

SPIRIT OF THE EAGLE

Lift your spirits and let them soar, on eagles' wings
o'er mountain peaks
Where kestrels fly, and snow lies cold, and the white hare dances
spring,
Pause and rest by a shimmering stream, where kingfishers swoop
and dive.
Touch your ears with bird song sweet, heralding hope and fresh
new life
Scent the perfume of blossoms fair, and fresh cut grass after
gentle rain
Wonder now at the Universe, shooting stars, Comet and Milky Way
Comfort your mind with joyous thoughts, sunset, starlight and
moon-drenched lakes
Feel the warmth of the sun on your face, and the fresh cool touch of
the rain
The glorious gift of autumn tints, and winter's blanket of soft
white snow
Think happy, think joyful, think words of light, and fly with the eagle
o'er mountains high.

C M Bellamy

TOP WITHINS

Did this old farmhouse fire the wild imaginary place
where Heathcliff and Cathy ran,
now piled stone bricks where tourists come
to eat their sandwiches,
sit singly, or in married ranks
as a camera clicks?

New-found friends, in deepest *agape,*
we see no ghosts,
cut no conventions,
throw no stones,
ponder how to live excised by circumstance
from what moved Cathy and Heathcliff.

We go, stick to the footpath,
leave Howarth Moor behind,
hug hurriedly at the train
and say Goodbye.

Wise words linger like a kindly lie
as loneliness returns,
is yours, and, somewhere else, is mine,
and now those ghosts move soundlessly
into the mind's eye,
run over rock and stone,
charge the potency of earth,
and now we know that place
more lasting than Top Withins
called Wuthering Heights.

Justin Barnard

Fellow Traveller
(For James Cameron)

I am a dancer. I write about dance.
I'm a tightrope walker
on the brink,
hovering inside and outside,
drawn by curiosity,
the spark of the new,
swept up by the eagerness of others
clamouring to tell their tale.
I stumble into conversation
seeking the keen moment,
to seize it with a slow shutter
then let it fly: a new take
bursting with the texture of the original;
empathetic but on guard,
ready to jolt from intimacy to distance,
a sated boxer refuelling between bouts,
clutching at stray hints:
clues murmuring beneath the surface
that break through to illuminate the exchange.
Assimilation: the Director's Cut -
an instant colour wash over a mass of grey dots
waving flags from a stony island.
Drawing attention to the intricate energy of others,
the slow flood of creativity that warms the world,
I'm charged.
Sometimes I flag,
ensnared by the tumult of voices
but am revived by the zest of fellow travellers
trying the same high-wire.

Norma Cohen

ONCE YOUR WIFE

Do you remember, the golden band
You placed 'so lovingly' upon my hand?
Then, we were so very happy,
Never arguing, or getting snappy.
Our days were filled with so much love,
And I was your little turtle dove.
Remember the nights, that were heaven-sent,
I now sit and wonder . . . where they all went.
Echoes of children, filled the house,
We once were happy, me and my spouse.
Oh, why do people drift apart?
When, all that's left, is a broken heart.
I remember, on our Wedding day . . .
Kneeling, and holding hands to pray,
Vows, we made . . . to stay together.
We thought that it would last forever.
But now, we seem, like worlds apart,
Both sat nursing a broken heart.
We are filled with such remorse,
As the date approaches . . . for our divorce.
So sad, our love, came to an end,
And now, you've just become a friend.
And although, I once, became your wife,
I regret . . . it didn't last for life.
But I know, that there will always be . . .
A special place, inside of me,
Where your memory, will linger on,
And stay, until my days are gone.

Deana Houghton

Untitled

When I get to the promised land
Will St Peter say to me,
'What have you done for men on earth?'
Not much you must agree.

What of the poems that I wrote,
Will they not count I'll say?
They will give pleasure to people,
Long after my dying day.

What have they done for your fellow man,
Healed his wounds says he,
Have they fed the poor and hungry,
have they set the prisoner free?

From somewhere; a voice I heard,
Saying poetry has its worth,
If it had not been for writers,
Who would have known of us on earth?

C E Cannon

Quietness

Everyone needs quietness just to rest our mind.
We all should try and have this just for us to unwind.
We shouldn't be dashing about every minute of the day.
If we keep on like this our health will certainly pay.

It is nice sometimes to be busy and have constructive things to do.
But we must get the balance right - it is only up to you.
Just put your feet up or read a favourite book, that is a good idea.
Read a happy calming story - not one where you shed a tear.

Take the phone off the hook for one hour or two.
Then you won't be disturbed - it will be good for you.
You will be a happier person the rest of the day.
Don't feel guilty about it - it's your life, you have to say.

To get the benefit do this regularly.
A calmer, more well-balanced person you will turn out to be.
Remember - always running here and there is a bat habit to start.
Rest as well as play will look after your heart.

Edith Meldrum Cooke

FAITH

Faith is but a heartbeat away,
Is just a mystery,
Like night turns into day,
Faith shows what is good,
In everyone,
And shows the world,
In such a gentle way,
When each day is done.

So let there be another source,
Of understanding,
That shows us all,
There are many ways,
That we can find peace,
Within our hearts,
And lose all the nastiness,
Before it has time to start.

Colin Hush

TO LIVE ONE DAY ON EARTH

Awake and face the dawn of day
With thought set out to please,
Cast out the doubt, no need to shout,
There's plenty cause to tease

Give tenderness to those in need
A smile along the way,
A cheeky story to your friends
With time set out for play

Today is here to live it well
It won't repeat for sure,
So work on it and make it real
Enjoy life to the core

Your mind is so uniquely yours
No two are made the same,
Make out to use it your own way
And play out life's long game

Throughout the day seek things anew
Play music, tend a flower,
Whatever turns you on do well
Employ your every hour

When turning to your bed at night
look upward to the sky
And thank the Lord above right then
The day's not passed you by

Tomorrow is a sleep away
You'll rest well in your bed,
And those around will read your mind
Then arms will widely spread.

Sam Royce

WHEN YOU'RE GONE

When you're gone
Don't stop to wonder if we ever
Think of you.
The same moon shines
The same wind blows.
For all of us in time is
but a paper moon be not gone

So when you're gone
As if we hold a flower
That touches you be not gone
A new life grows.

When you're gone
The blossom knows because no-one
else could warm our
Hearts as much as you
Be not gone.

When you're gone
Let us cling together and die
As the year goes.
By oh not god
Be not gone.

When you're gone
Don't stop to wonder if we
Look at you and listen
And learn or follow from your
Steps.
By our god
Be not gone.

Joanne Ramsden (15)

SOCIAL CLASSES

Money gathered in its masses
Won't be based on social classes
Rich people won't be elitist
Because others don't become defeatist
Working class men are determined
To ill fortune not be pinned
He will break out from his root
In the end he'll have as much loot

God made all men equal
But some unfortunates were forced down
Rich persons acted so cruel
When they kicked these people around
The justice of life was raped
The benevolence of life was faked
labelled peasants struggled so hard
To rebuild their backyards

Rich people can't be complacent
Because we're hot onto their scent
Genes haven't watered down our brains
No class can turn off our mains
We shall match them in the end
Equal them all my dear friends
The Almighty will be pleased
When snobbery will soon be ceased.

Tay Collicutt

THE WIND'S DISCORDANT BALL

Branches chortle excitedly,
in a laughing group.
Flowers in beds cringe,
in a servile stoop.

Hanging washing swings,
in non-sequence dance.
Old gardeners' wispish locks,
gyrate in disco prance.

A rocking, creaking fence,
in wood stained coat,
forced to emit
a cacophonous note.

Plant pots topple,
crash and clatter,
with unharmonious
non-resonant chatter.

A parachuting dandelion seed
in fermented, turbulence flies,
desperate to land before
from destruction it dies.

A captive audience
in the garden bound,
responds with movement
and vociferous sound.

Ken Ford

GAP BRIDGING THE WORLD

A united Britain,
Europe united too
When islands are linked
By bridges, tunnels too

If they can unite
France to England by rail
They should build a link to the Isle of Wight
Surely this can't fail

Or perhaps they could try to connect
England to the Isle of Man
Or even build a tunnel to Ireland
I wonder if they can?

All the Scottish islands
Orkney and Shetland too
Connected to the mainland
By bridge or tunnel too

I hope one day all islands
Could be linked together this way
No need to wait for ferries
To take us on our way!

H G Griffiths

BE PATIENT

But oh be kind have patience
Hide your temper with a smile
For the aged can be with us
Such a little while.

Once they were young and fearless too
With strong and steady hands
But now they have all kinds of dread.
that no-one understands, try and give them confidence
Not turn a look that's cold
Remember other people too
Will need patience when you're old.

Julie Allwright

MEXICO CITY

Welcoming, overwhelming Mexico City
too warm by day, too cold at night
Cars, dirt, noise, fumes, crowds
eating, chatting, selling; loud!
Never-ending crowds,
variegated multitudes,
from dark sculptured Indians
to white, the mighty.

Eighteen million
squeezing along together
with more apparent tolerance
than most overcrowded cities.
Amazing, the order they create:
neat piles of fruit, watered streets, quiet queues
innate sense of right which the powerful abuse.

So many women, overdressed, ugly-pretty;
the poorest squat on pavements, resigned underclass
while Americans admire vast Marxist frescoes,
modern metro, mammoth churches; paradox city.

Olga Kenyon

HOME-MADE WINE

In summer and winter with a friend I combine
Turning windfall apples into home-made wine
We've a potent recipe as imbibers attest
Advisedly drunk only before a nap or a rest

We've both won prizes at a local flower show
The wine class judge surely felt a bit of a glow
Never mind the Sauvignon, Chianti, Rioja or Hock
Our wine is British from home-grown apple stock

In order that drivers are not led astray
They're supplied with a home brew 'takeaway'
We like sharing results of our labours with friends
We know those who prefer 'sweet' or 'dry' blends

In winter demi-johns echo with plopping sounds
In spring there's a sediment of spent yeast grounds
Next we siphon off the clear wine with a chance to try
The taste of the vintage, be it sweet or be it dry

When my mum in her 80s made home brew in a crock
It was I who tried it and tended to mock
Little knowing that one day a winemaker I'd be
With modern equipment making the task easy for me

Yvonne Smith

MOVING ON

Drink deeply of my body,
for our time is almost over.
My love is on the wane now,
So you may not have it long.

Our time was very special,
and I would never change it.
But the cycle is complete now,
and I'm ready to move on.

Lesley Kate Mitchell

What Is A Soul?

The light in your eyes
The smile that glows
The existence of life
That is a soul

The candlelight burning
The moonlight so pale
The stars ever shining
That is a soul

The meaning of life
The shining within
No one should doubt
This shell we live in

When it is time
To depart from this life
The soul ever shining
So pure and so bright
Will leave this cold body
And fly to the skies
To join the stars shining
So high and so bright

Elsa M Summers

REFLECTIONS

Even though I'm far away,
My thoughts are with you every day.
And err the sun has gone to rest,
I think of home, far away to the west.

The evenings I had strolling in the park,
Or chasing about with the dog before dark.
Easy strokes in a boat on the lake,
Drifting awhile when my arms did ache.

Folks playing bowls on the lawn so green,
These things come back, as if in a dream.
Men nearby at the game of draughts,
A winning move, a silent laugh.

Old people resting on the seats
Admiring young people, trim and neat.
Or, discussing the fun they had in their day,
As homeward they plodded their weary way.

Walking through town on a Saturday night,
The shows aglow in a blaze of light.
And shouts in the market of men at the stalls,
Reaching beyond those sombre walls.

Sunday evenings, when the band did play,
In that band-stand that's so far away.
Music sad, mostly bright, wafting on the shades of night,
When peace and quietness did reign,
O'er the music's dying strain.

St Margaret's Church, the pealing bells,
These were the things I knew so well,
Before I left the town of my birth,
To begin my travels o'er this war-torn earth.

I cherish these dreams of things to come,
Once more to my life when peace is won.
Far from this air, laden with sand,
Back to England, my home, and my land.

Denis Holgate

HEADS HIGH, AS THE ORCHESTRA PLAYED TILL THE END

Beholding no risk as the maiden sailed,
Cutting the film of the brim of marine,
Some minutes late as the deserters wailed,
As mist pulled apart fortune true was foreseen.

Vigourful life is unspoilt as fresh snow,
Accustoms grow fonder as heart follows trend,
Refreshing new changes from lost styles once known,
Material minds of the rich never mend.

A smooth sail cut short as a death or a murder,
An iceburg as a knife or such lying in wait,
patriarchs panic as solely waves heard her,
Material minds of the rich never mend.

Lonely lifeboats lowered into the lush aquatic sheet,
Silent prayers, glassy stares, and guilt felt to survive,
A bond grows in the ocean as the ship and still bed meet,
Realise, with sad goodbyes, fortune to be alive.

The unsinkable ship contradicted its name,
Slated was luxury and comfort intend,
Morale was kept high, as honour filled the sky,
Heads high, as the orchestra played till the end.

Katie Prentice

TOGETHER AGAIN

Lightning struck
At the moment we kissed
Our thoughts were so full
Of the things we had missed
Our hearts were so frail
Our hands held so strong
Our lost time apart
Was far too long
The sky clapped with thunder
So heavy the rain
Once more we kissed
Together again.

Melvyn Roiter

THE MEADOWS

Cobwebs, like gossamer lace,
In early morning mist
Dew upon the waking flowers
As night, turns into day.
Calling of the songbirds
Heralds the new day,
Everywhere, there's beauty
If we would slow our pace
To look around instead of race,
And take
        one day at a time!
To give us space
Instead of rushing
        at a busy pace.

M Parnell

MAX'S MOP

I've known my friend Maxine for several years
We've had lots of laughs and shed a few tears
But the cause of most of her concern and care
Is her crowning glory, her barnet, her hair

The lengths have been varied and the style's changed too
And she always has worries let me tell you
She grew out her fringe after several tries
Then chopped it right off 'cos it got in her eyes

'I need much more volume' we all heard her cry
As she's off to the hairdressers a diffuser to buy
'Heated rollers I think would give me more lift -
Or a professional hairdryer I'd love as a gift'

Her tongs like to travel, they're essential you see
When you're hiking in Ireland or on safari
On lotions and potions she's spent lots of dosh
Hairsprays and mousses and shampoo - frequent wash!

The perms have been plenty but just not quite right
'Do you think it's too frizzy, too curly, too tight?'
'I'll try one for body to just get a kink -
Oh no it has dropped much too soon don't you think?'

And now she has highlights and we think it sure suits
But she checks every day if we've noticed her roots
Her hairdresser should get an achievement award
For with Max as a customer she's never been bored

But enough is enough, no more must I dig
I've saved up enough now to buy her a wig
And she really shouldn't worry or get in a state
'Cos whenever I see her she always looks great!

Dawn Potter

JORDAN

With healing love you came
sky blue eyes, winning smile.
Clear as a bell
your love
smote our hearts
and made them sing again
Broke free -
the binding chains of life,
and weary hearts loved -
in ecstasy.

With healing smiles you brought
gladness to our souls,
joy and laughter, hopes and dreams
of a future yet to come.
But in your joyous giving
a bitter pill resides,
the price we pay for loving
a growing up - denied.
In that brief life a reckoning
as the flame of love died.

We are spirit soul and body
they tell us in the church,
and your Soul Light ascended
to the All Light of God.
The message you have left us
is that soul and spirit came
to record and experience
in an earthly frame.
And like the fleeting feelings
of an ever-wakening heart
our soul and spirit, are of us,
an integrated part.

You came in 'Trails of Glory'
from your home beyond the skies.
You accomplished your earth mission
and returned, to summarise,
your brief life here on earth,
in the love you freely gave,
and shower still upon us
from beyond the earthly grave.

Irene Di Mascio

EMPTY I AM

I lie on the pillow, the tears fill my eyes,
Lying on the pillow for the missing of love,
Crying on the pillow, longing for its coming,
Dying on the pillow lest it never comes,
Teardrops welling to drown hidden sorrow,
Beckoning and calling love to come to me,
I've done my chores, their emptiness tears me,
The quietness saddens my feelings unconsoled,
Left alone, abandoned, forgot on a whim,
Lying all alone, comfortless bar my pillow,
In distance music plays in my heart it does not,
Melodies and dulcet tones pour over my ears,
Taunting but not touching the sadness within,
Misery, rejection abound this empty shell,
Depression claws the mind tearing the heart,
As I lie alone on the pillow, alone in life.

Paul Hetherington

THE BETTER WAY

I'd rather see a sermon
    Than to hear one any day.
I'd rather one should walk with me,
    Than merely show the way.
The eyes are better pupils,
    And more willing than the ear,
Fine counselling is confusing,
    But an example is always clear.
And the best of all the preachers,
    Are the men who live their creeds,
For to see good put in action,
    Is what everybody needs.
I can watch your hands in action,
    But your tongue too fast may run,
And the lectures you deliver,
    May be very wise and true.
But I'd rather get my lesson
    By observing what you do,
For I may misunderstand you,
    And the high advice you give,
But there's no misunderstanding in
    How you act and how you live.

William Price

THE MOTHER AND CHILD RELATIONSHIP

The baby cried, her mother gently rocked her.
She snuggled her to her breast and fed her.
What peace and comfort, for both mother and child.
How long will this precious moment last.
Would war, famine or pestilence break this bond.

For what is the price of peace and harmony.
Can success, power or money comfort a child.
Does not love, hope and goodwill endure.
This relationship will survive the test of time.
Like gold its beauty is eternal.

K A Davis

MORE RESPECT

We should pay the greatest respect to her
Majesty the Queen. If we search all over
The world we would never find anyone who can
Match the Queen of England. I do understand
That some people are upset with the
Royals and the monarchy. I am not
Surprised after the newspaper and the
Media splashed out for a long time
They really changed the people's mind.
I do not think that England would be
Better off if the monarchy one day
Will go. The people of England
They still do not know how lucky
They are, to have a great Queen.
We must praise and give more
Respect of the highest esteem
To her Royal Majesty.
She's served this country very well
From a very young princess. I hope
That the queens and kings will forever
Stand for the security and
The future of England!
Long live the Royal Family!

Antonio Martorelli

WHO?

Who was it who called the battle cry
Who was it who left the soldier to die
Who was it who made the young man sigh
For the life he was denied
Who was it who had the darling mother/wife
Lie sleepless in the night for want or try
Who was it who widowed the mother
Orphaned the child
Bereft the family with no goodbye
Who was it and for what reason why?

Fitzlillian

THE WORLD CUP REGATTA, MUNICH, JUNE 1977

So Redgrave and Pinsent are in the news
with Foster and Cracknell they've found the right crews!

Their training
and straining
has paid off quite well
Their rowing has showed us
They've a story to tell!

They were strong and bold
As they took the 'gold'!

Marie Barker

HAPPY BIRTHDAY JULIET

I am my family, as Romeo I stand,
Beneath your balcony in a far-off land.
We gaze at your photo of which I behold,
Never before has beauty's story been told.

You are out little girl in a funny sort of a way.
Yet you are not belonging, by Birth, or through Marriage? Nay.
Someday our two families will meet.
Not at war or through hate, where killing and famine are evil's victory,
But through love and friendship and trust.
Where we care, though we have not seen, or have not talked, or
                                                                       listened to.
Where colour, or creed, or religion prevent.
Where God's angel rules and not Evil's serpent.

Maybe? Someday who knows? Romeo and Juliet will be as one.
In a world void of hurt and pain.
Where the rain of happiness soothes all.
Where there is no asking, only sharing.
Where there is laughter and not children crying.
Where I give before you ask.
Where you thank before I give.
Where we all share equally in the word we call Life.

Oh Juliet my little one, be there distance further than the eye can see
between my family as Romeo and your family called Juliet.
Maybe in the end our story of love will end only in happiness and
not the Fabled tragedy.

James Thomas Hopkins

NEVER LET IT HAPPEN AGAIN

The man I loved
A monster he became
With lies and deceit he destroyed me
My life no longer worth living
A drink to face the next day
A black hole I'd fallen in
No one could help me.
Excuses I made, lies I told, was just not me!
What had happened to me
I was used and abused
The knife in deep being twisted
I still kept clean
My love for him would not die
Left to skin and bone no life of my own
No one could help me
I hear you call 'What a fool'
But my love for him would not die.
The mirror I passed one day
Who's that lady old and grey?
It's me, what a sorry state to be in
Responsibility he'd left behind
I crawled in the hole all alone
Painted a smile when I wanted to cry
That day I started to live once more
The scar cut deep, what a fool I've been.
Lesson learned *never let it happen again.*

Christine Davis

ANGER TRAPPED

Trapped inside this body
trapped inside this mind
trapped inside these memories.
Talking doesn't help
speaking doesn't free
nothing seems to ease
the pain of being me.

Cramped inside this gut
waiting to explode
don't want to walk this journey
don't want to walk this road.

Tears inside my stomach
gushing out with rage
rip out this diseased heart
that's tearing me apart.

Destroy this angry body
silence this noisy mind
leap into oblivion
and leave it all behind.

But the dark subsides
light starts to glimmer through
the dam that burst inside
is trickling out of view.

Ellen Cooper

WOMANHOOD

He hated the smiles that she smiled at him,
he could read them like a map, he knew what
was behind them, the sickly smiles were the
worst, she couldn't fool him anymore.

She murdered him with her womanhood, she
was like a cup of oversweet tea, he liked
the way she moved inside that dress, but he
hated himself for it because he had become
her slave and she knew it; she was an
artist of the art of womanhood.

K J Herbert

WORK TOGETHER

We must all work together
That's what we all must do
Be environmentally friendly
In everything we do
Look after the rivers
Look after the seas
Take care of the meadows
Take care of the trees
Save the elephant
Save the whale too
We must all work together
That's what we all must do

Alan Green

I Believe In This Earth

I believe in this earth,
Its bounteous wonders to perceive,
Scenic views to glory on
Produce there for food.
Climates rich and wonderful
Heady with perfume,
Or cold and crisp all year.
Marvels of nature everlasting.
Architectural man-made structures
Reaching for the sky.

I believe in this earth
Its many races,
Mixing with each other
Sharing skills.
Helping one another
During their short stay
Showing that they care.

I believe in this earth
Its purpose everlasting,
In seasons changing
Nature knows its duty.
Would man learn its reasoning,
Cease destruction
Of God's creation?

I believe in this earth,
And human nature.
Living as intended
Tending to its needs
All in harmony.
Force world-wide
Cease to have a meaning
Parley - parley
If you must.

Jack Allerston

I M - R S Thomas

With language learnt from an unearthed skull
                    with a stone tongue
still soil-stained, its shine taken by the clay
robbed and redacted from the tombs of
          Llandogo, Llanigon, Llansilin, Llan-y-pwell,
ap-Williams, ap-Jones, ap-Tudor, ap-Thomas
anybody, nobody,
Neb

the poet speaks furiously
in his mother's voice, breast-fed vowels
under an English cloak
in a London suburb

his own history
of being a lion in a dragon's skin

under the larkwing in the voiceless air

Andrew Hawthorne

The Palaces Of The Anti Hero

Alas, this wanton power-play, me above you.
Floored you are to the marbled palace
of the anti-hero
Where near certain creeping death
and everlasting depths of my anger
screen the silent smoking vaults
of historic bone collections.
Labyrinths of absinthe
dyes of redness
and this killing joke.

Mark Hemingway

First Love

I remember the first time I held you in my arms;
I could feel your soft, warm body next to me,
And hear the gentle beating of your heart.
You didn't realise that your arrival transformed my world forever;
I began to live for your happiness alone,
Doing anything to please you, anything to win your love.
And when I stared into your deep brown eyes I would see our future:
Togetherness, indefinitely spanning time.

Days soon became weeks, weeks became months and years;
I became closer and closer to you.
I was always by your side,
Sharing with you the same sorrow, the same joy,
And the same immeasurable love
That created the idyllic moments I cherished.
I remember the long, lazy afternoons spent in the garden,
And the beautiful array of flowers you picked for me;
Posies that did not wither and die, but grew forever in my heart.

Then one day you told me you were leaving.
I had always known that you would,
Yet knowing the inevitable did not lessen the pain.
I had to let you go;
Though I felt like I was losing a part of myself,
I could never stand in the way of your dreams.
But remember my darling, wherever you are, whatever you do,
A mother's love remains constant and true.

Zahra Lalani

DEATH OF INNOCENCE

A war is a destructive creature.
It will take lives on demand,
It has no compassion,
No forgiveness or mercy.
The innocence it feeds on is pure,
Defenceless without hope.
Do you think the children cry,
When their mothers don't come home?
When their fathers don't bring food,
Do you think their bellies hurt?
This animal *'they'* call war,
Will spread throughout the world.
As bombs begin to drop,
And the snipers start to shoot.
Do the children see those bodies fly,
And imagine they're ragdolls?
As the innocence they're born with,
turns to rage and anger,
Do you think those children realise,
They're children of the war?
As the boys play with their guns,
Mirroring armed soldiers.
Do the girls look up with pride,
or simply cry?
This war is a destructive creature,
Yet its children will fight on.
A voice from within is heard,
Who will love my children,
When Mother Nature's gone?

Dionne Lindsay

SELF-PSYCHOANALYSIS

I retired at forty, due to illness.
I wrote down everything I ever did.
In the absence of psychotherapy,
I made notes, articles, and poems,
and read through my diaries.
One of my best travelogues
was written while mentally ill!
I studied, when I could, various subjects,
from astrology to psychiatry, and relaxed
with yoga. Now, I know my ups and
downs, and continue, avoiding pressure,
to take an interest in life, and people.
Van Gogh was schizophrenic, probably.
He couldn't have done his paintings
if he'd been on suppressive drugs!
While these help me, I feel
my emotions curbed. Maybe time
will burn-up the burn-out.

Keith Murdoch

A THOUGHT FOR TODAY

Sometimes when I have to go away
there's something which I always remember.
That no matter where I am
Or whatever path I choose to walk on through life,
There's one path I have already chosen,
that will always lead me back to you.

Bernadette C Curran

Eye In The Sky

High above our planet's
polluted atmosphere
the eye in the sky
scans the seas of space
gathering the pulsing starlight
which it absorbs and transmits
to us and we can convert
into symbols we can understand
and use to expand our knowledge.

It penetrates space
looking at happenings
trillions of light years ago . . .
back to the Big Bang
when our universe was formed
from nothing in a blazing birth -
no matter, no time, no space, no life
existed until the baby cosmos
was safely delivered in a microsecond.

And finally we hope
the seeing eye
will show us
the starway to infinity
beyond the fringe
of space and time . . .
the powerhouse dimension
of the cosmic mover . . .
the creator.

Stephen Gyles

THE BLOOD-RED HAND

The blood-red hand of Ulster
That taints St George's cross
Waves high upon its flagpole
Where the loyal orders scoff
This union of mockeries
A pact conceived in hell
A chamber full of tortures
In which death's the sweetest smell

A handshake with the devil
Leaves its mark upon the land
And every politician
Has fresh blood upon his hands
Where honour wears a veil of lies
For truth is gagged and bound
And thud of soil on coffin
Is the punctuating sound

The blood-red hand of Ulster
That grips St George's cross
Waves boldly from its flagpole
Unashamed of lives it's cost
Hypocrisy still casts its brush
Upon this cursed scene
Where peace is but a metaphor
That Loyalist Rule be gleaned

Kim Montia

EVERY

Don't dream
if you can't be bothered to live it
it's all very well looking at a cake
but it's something else to eat it all
Never mumble when you want to scream

Don't laugh
if to be laughed at twists your mouth
To slip over may hurt delicate limbs
but to then cry would only hurt more
anything else doesn't register above a half

Don't bleed
if the acceptance of this sweet elixir
makes you shy of other substances
each urge is instinctive and honest
or as true as the potential of a seed

Can't sleep
then the world dries your every pore
with the seconds that feed you
and one hour seems wholly wasted
in sleep's dark evil of a keep

Don't walk
if you don't see the explicit irony
of being not in control of ourselves
but led by the iron rusted chains
we accept with every word we talk

Andy McPheat

The Green - Cambridge
Early Spring

Edging The Green, in transport of delight
A single almond tree, dressed and showy
For the spring, shook sadly its tresses.
Beyond the brook, slow-running o'er the mud
Of winter, grew luscious grass, bog-born
Which thrived indifferent to the burgeoning
Of the season's early warmth. People
On The Green, arms close-linked and talking
Did not see the lovely almond tree
Gently beckoning, nor feel the quivering
In the air nor hear the shrill of birdsong,
Nor watch the blue sky spreading at the parting
Of the clouds, white as the fleece of lambs.

Elizabeth Hampden

Divine...

I n a flash she said
N o help was needed,
S omeone supplied a
P oem on life.
I didn't write it, it's not even my style
R ead it again and take notice,
A message is hidden in
T hese words.
I nspiration from heaven above,
O Lord help me treasure and
N ever forget your wonders and your love.

Suzanne Woolner

TERRESTRIAL SHELLS

An hour from walking barefoot on your grass
- I watched the stream there, and the rain
Scooped in hollows
I remembered other eyes, another voice
The bony sockets of old and new love
Dried out like sheep skulls on the hills -
What are terrestrial shells?
I need only imagine fragility
Wafered layers of egg-blue
Powdering into nothing, like love
Yet leaving their echoes
As a song
Their soft shapes
Massed in dark exchanges
Under the hills

Elizabeth Ashworth

WORKLESS

Depression walks my mind
My love. I see not you or
Our children, only my
Loss of pride. Will the
Pills return me to you
Once again, only time can
Tell. Will they restore
My hope, my pride, my
Mind to me.

A Smart

RICHARD III AT THE FILM SOCIETY

Showing at the local centre, cosy, friendly
(The utilitarian space, wobbly seats
Shared like silly kids' secrets),
It comes on out-of-focus.
The projectionist adjusts

Ineffectually - it doesn't matter
And won't for the duration:
The direction is knife-clean
Like the 40s Fascist costumes;
And the iambic pentameters

Are fully clipped and bonded
As on the South Bank.
Ian McKellan is a well hunched gem
Coruscating every syllable and wink:
My Maggie (Smith) sparkles and

Crackles speech-squibs through assumed old age.
The battle trains, steam locomotives,
Horses and Battersea Power Station
Lack only real Meccano
And boy-manipulators

For complete conviction.
None of the horror and terror is lost -
Evil and good as clear as ever
(The former more compelling, as usual) -
And the projector's clatter, the pop

And crunch of refreshments, the snap
And loose-end flap of the film
Half-way through does nothing
To distract the Bard's ghost's
Approving chuckles in the front row.

F L Bramah

Shattered

I paint my life on a large piece of glass.
I use many colours. I mix and blend,
Hoping for the perfect result.

The paint dries and I admire my work,
Holding it up to the light for maximum colour effect.
I rejoice as the sun shines through the colours I have created.
I am pleased with the result.
Satisfied.
At peace with my creation.

All of a sudden the glass is shattered.
Unseen forces have destroyed my creation,
So fragile in its physical construction
Yet so strong and important to me.

Who could have done this?
I complain loudly, bemoaning my loss.
What could motivate someone to destroy
Such a treasured creation
Belonging to someone else?

There can be many reasons for the breakage -
Malice, bereavement, error, a change in circumstances.
The tides of life sweep us up from time to time
And crash us against a rough sea wall.
We can feel ourselves crumble as we lie there,
Shattered and soaked.

The reasons are not important.
But the fact must be faced that a life has been shattered.
A million colourful pieces of glass are scattered
Far and wide across the earth.

But, just a moment,
It broke so easily.
So little force was required to wipe out
Years of persistent effort, treasured beliefs and memories.

Was it really worth it? Hadn't I better start again?
My creation has been shattered but I am still here.
So I get out my paintbox of ideas and I begin again.

Anne-Marie Whitwell

A Way Out

For you death was a way out
but did you ever think of me?
You left me wondering what it was all about
I did not understand why you wanted to die
As you were lying there
While ambulance men beside you knelt
And tried to wake you up?
Did you give a thought to me?
When I watched them take you away
How could you fail to see
All the confusion and fear?
Why did you keep going away
When inside you knew
That I would grow up more each day
because I was used as a substitute for you?

Kim Harrison

ACACIA AVENUE

On the pavement
kids on tricycles go round in circles,
mothers' arms folded chin-wag
the days away

Whilst short-sleeved
men gather under car bonnets,
buttocks hung out
like Las Vegas
slot machines.

String-vested old
men creosote garden fences -
one eye on the evening's
dominoes game
- home banker.

The sun spilt
out till midnight
never going
down until every last
good 'un home
kisses the tarmac -
God bless 'em all I say
and all that sail
in her.

G C Freeth

SPIN DOCTOR

Spin doctor, wistfully manipulating, toeing the party line.
Making sure their employers are under the one design.
Media are here, the lights shine bright as they crave the latest
sound-bite.

PR delights, the faceless ghouls with the bland pork faces.
Spin faster doctor, in the hope people will believe,
Is it the *truth?* Who *cares?*
As long as it sounds right so here comes the latest *Sh-t* . . .

Duncan Campbell

HOUSE OF GOD

The church door was open.
It seemed so inviting and a magnet pulled.
I remembered times long ago,
As a kid when I sang solo,
'Good King Wenceslas' soprano.
The panto's, church hall, Mother Goose.
Putting out chairs and dressing up on Sundays.
A whole way of life, a sense of belonging,
Of being a part.

But the door although open
And the magnet although pulling
Could not attract me in and I felt fear.
A feeling of betrayal.
I remembered the bishop
Who knew my father on first name terms,
I remembered my own Confirmation
But still the door was not open wide enough
To allow me to understand.

I wanted then to apologise, to whom I do not know,
a friend perhaps who I had hurt and who in turn had hurt me.
And finally I drew myself away.
Knowing all along I never intended to go in.
But always wishing that I had.

Tony Jones

THE DOWNSIDE OF DEMOCRACY!

I voted for him last time.
I have seen him since
Smug in his safe seat.
I have heard him braying from a back bench
At some unwitty jibe
Not because it was funny,
But because it was spoken by an honourable member from *his* side
To the discomfiture of an honourable member from the other

Maybe I should vote for his opponent this time,
Chosen by the party faithful
Not for his values,
Nor for his sincerity,
But because he is a vote winner:
A charmer

Her then?
The political woman
With carefully lowered tones
And ruthlessly managed hair -
Holding her place in a man's world.
Austere and daunting.

How can I bring myself to vote for those who do not believe
That they can make mistakes:
Self-believers,
Political types
Sacrificed on the altar of their chosen party agenda?

Whoever I vote for,
Will assume
That just like their party sheep
I support their *every* move.
My cross will never voice my reservations.

I might give my vote for party A
To rescue my children's education
Only to find myself guilty
Of destroying
The nation's health.
Or I could vote for party B,
Strong on law and order,
And by default give them licence to destroy the nation's economy!
We only have the freedom
To choose between the choices of others.

And this is the down-side of democracy:
Those who vote
Have only themselves to blame.

Barbara J Parsons

AND THERE WAS LOVE

When it was all over
I tried to sleep
But couldn't.
Images of the past
Became the present.
And there was no future.
There were yesterdays
But no tomorrows,
There were children
But no adults,
There were delinquents
But no policemen,
And there was love
But no you.

Tony Jones

Nunc Dimittis

Now O Lord my labours are complete
Your glory shone through my transient life
and now the wonder of creation is renewed.

Now I behold with vicarious pride
that Sabbath peace and totality of rest
which transcends time to eternity.

B J Bramwell

First Kiss

A tingle down my spinal cord
a hand sliding down my hair
it sent me everso dizzy
like I was floating in the air.

That day was special and perfect
not a cloud was up above
when at that moment I realised
I had fallen deep in love.

My parents said I'd gone all soppy
my friends said it would not last
but our feelings are still there
even though two years have passed.

I think it was that special moment
when I had that tingle down my spine
when it sent me everso dizzy
when I realised he was mine.

Amanda Lawrence (15)

ALIENS

Rising from the mire
It let out a high-pitched scream
And low rumblings
Silver liquid bubbling from its casing
Vaporising in the thin atmosphere
Drifting towards the other
Whose snapping tendons signalled readiness
Running gold droplets of desire
Vibrating hotly as a tentacle reached out
Wrapped around
Pulling them together
Silver into gold
Latticeworks locking
Gushing cloud enveloping
Running acids
Hydro-carbons
Igniting
A chemical catalyst
That flared violently for micro seconds
Melting, fusing
High-pitched screams
Erupting from the furnace
That quickly cooled
The union over
They flopped back down into the hot mud
Smoking.

Robert Godfrey

THE DREAM

My lately deceased father
came to me in a dream:
the most hideous sight
I have ever seen.
Direct from the grave,
he appeared to have come,
his sudden presence
struck me dumb -
half-decomposed and dripping
flesh, with sightless
sockets and decaying breath.
Through months of remorse
filled, fitful nights I had
mourned my father's death;
brooding on what I
wished I'd said,
while helplessly watching
him gasping for life,
as he lay on his hospital bed.
Words that might have
gently soothed the mutually
inflicted and still weeping
sores where we rubbed each
other the wrong way;
seeing in his ceasing to be
my own inevitable mortality;
yet unable to accept the finality
of his predestined demise.
Now he stood before me,
in some awful disguise.
I began to gabble, and in
my distress, confessed my
feelings and all the affection
I'd failed to express.

The phantom listened: then,
with a satisfied, sepulchral
sigh, the presence left.
And peace of mind prevailed.

Jeremy Gadd

THE PEACE OF SINKING YOUR HEAD IN THE BATH

There are times when I am Me and Me's at peace.

I wash the dust of the day from my eyes.
The girl's pretty face. The girl's little lies.
Are out of my mind.

I'm by myself.

I rinse the gust of the day from my mouth.
Friends expect this. And others the rest.
It's senseless.

I sink my head back.

The hot water claps a silk veneer over my ears.
If I'm less in time. Well they tried their best.
The silence caresses.

This is a brief reprieve.

From the sweat and the murder. From being killed further.
There are times when I am Me and Me's at peace.
Only in the bath and when I'm asleep.

Ross Styants

CHARRED

Drunk faced and
red nosed
I sit and listen
to the dead
beats rattle on
unsure and wary
of their songs
in this lonely
loveless empty
town
Outside
past the streets
full of trees
the empty beer cans
and the used condoms
the moon leers down
deacon of the
desolation
Something's wrong
with the world
all the coins are gone
from a poor boy's pockets
leaving holes behind
the city is empty
only the glazed
lepers remain
in the ruins
and the scaffolding
the rubble
and the soot
of the night
and no-one seems to care
anymore
about anything
except themselves
and the next problem

my mind is torn
as I kiss the face
of the radio's voice
and hold
the empty hand
of the wind
blowing me
this way
that way
all across the land
seeing all the flypaper
hotels
all the sickness
all the ghouls
junkies nod out
waiting to be fixed
in telephone boxes
chain smoked
and cancer mouthed
I pick up all the pieces
of a broken man
before I sleep
and leave the world
to burn.

Michael Kemp

Love Is The Key

Every day people fussing and fighting.
We should get together and think about uniting.
Time's so short we should work our problems out
Think about our future don't leave our children in doubt.
With a little hard work and a lot of dedication
We could make it better for the next generation.
If people want to get things right
It's time we got together and stopped the fight.
Men killing men all over religion
Don't you think it's a funny situation?
Everybody knows there's only one God
He's in our hearts and He's about love.
If you really believe that love is a great sensation
Then we could get together and build a better nation.

David Brade

Time Passes

Tick, tock, tick

The time runs away, never to be seen again,
The history has been decided.
The time that you wasted, never to return,
You just watch it run and run.

  Tick, tock, tick

    Life just passing you by,
    Come back you cry, I've not finished.
    But time has gone.

    Tick, tock, tick

Daniel Laverty

At The End Of The Day

So . . . here we are, once again,
Wrapped in the blanket of turmoil,
that tomorrow will inevitably bring,
having bid 'Goodnight and God bless,'
to the precious fruits of our endeavours.
The children lying cocooned,
in their own private individual dreams,
oblivious to the fears and anguish,
from which we try desperately to safeguard them.
Thumbs gripped gently between cherubic lips,
fingers still entwined around silken locks of hair,
or clutching hems of their night clothes,
for comfort, against the dark unknown.
We stoop to kiss their small uncluttered heads,
and are ever amazed at the sudden relief of tension,
which is miraculously, though momentarily,
removed from our furrowed brows.
Alas the return to the real world,
is inevitably that brief moment away,
and we return to the old pervading stillness,
of the sombre night,
swathed once more in the grim realities,
from which we escaped,
for that precious sojourn into the awe-inspiring,
contentedness of our children's dreams.

Sleep tight little ones,
your dreams are your own,
but we are proud,
to be part of your fulfilment.

Des Billington

LOVE OF OUR LIFE

You came into our life a joy to behold
To make us happy as we grow old
You make us laugh as you dance and sing
You are our world our everything

The things that you can say and do
Never a moment is dull with you
You make each day seem even brighter
And make our nights seem even lighter

Your smile is like a breath of spring
We love to hear you laugh and sing
The joy to us you always bring
To you we wish for everything

When you appear you make our day
We hope that you are here to stay
Out come the toys, out come the dolls
And they are made to sit in the stalls

You dance and sing to all the dolls
And gramps is put in charge of the stalls
And if the dolls they do not clap
Grampa's put in charge of that

The joy and laughter that you bring
When we watch you dance and sing
We are certain of one thing
Upon the stage some day you'll sing

R M Campbell

Do You Love Me?

Why don't you say it?
Is it too hard to do?
They are only three small words
I and *love* and *you*

It takes a boy to be in a relationship
It takes a boy to say 'I do'
but it really takes a man
to say the words *I* and *Love* and *You*

So why don't you say it?
Is it too hard to do?
They are only three small words
I and *Love* and *You*

Amanda Lawrence (15)

A Spring Flower

Would nature a crocus had wished me to be,
to awaken the dawn when I would see, the sun in the
heaven's waiting to pass, to enhance my colours
that puts shame to the grass,
so envious since that last restful day, when did nature
with a smile on her face, cascade colour all over the place,
on her favourite the rainbow did most of it fall, while the
crocus, so patiently waiting her turn, was pleased when nature
did at last discern such promising beauty so early in spring,
then God, his work finished at last, suggested that with a canvas
so vast, she should use just one colour to paint the grass,
and ever since the eve of that day, after all God's creations had
been, she looked and searched all over the place,
but all she could find was green.

J Cuthbert

Full Moon Friday

Full moon Friday
I am on a high.
Seeing you on Saturday
I want to cry
out!

I could say nothing wrong
I made you laugh
At everything
And all the time.

'What has tickled you now?'
You asked.
And every time
Back you laughed.

Happy, sunny Saturday
Full moon Friday

Loved your company
Loved your mind
Who needs your bergamot
With me in full moon kind?

Sky clad
Moon clad
Grip me in your warm body
So lithe and young
Snuggleworthy body.

Full moon Friday
Saturday high
Just me
just you
your bed
and I am off into orbit

Full moons round my head.

Cath Simpkins

LIFE IS LIKE GEOMETRY!

Life is like geometry
It's full of corners!
And no one knows why these corners are there
Some are good
Some are bad
But all serve a purpose
Another link in the chain of life

Each day you turn new corners
Changing all the time
Learning through experience
Growing stronger every day

When things seem at their lowest
And you think you can take no more
Have the strength to turn that corner
You don't know what might be in store

Susan Oliver

HE NEVER WENT BACK

then Hurst was caught
with a bottle of whisky
at Queen Elizabeth's Boys School
the maths teacher took
the bottle off him
then Hurst was thrown
out of the school
he never went back
authority and school rules
he had simply broke
never to be let back
the others just smoke
those funny old fags
many were chain smokers
they could not be
hooked off it at all
so they still did it
the head teacher flew
into a long fit and
that teacher said he
must go to be punished
special school was the
one place for him
he was out of control
Hurst was a bully boy
all the women and the girls
he thought were his toys
just being a problem
all the time each day long

Richard Clewlow

First Wave

Now that I'm twenty-something
Past days of summer call me up
And reflect on me - but me not on them.

All too often they melt
The ice from the stick leaving a joke
I cannot confront.

Not so much skeletons
In the closet more bodies
In the field -

There are things we can't change
Things we can't make amends for.

Situation, time, spontaneity - *beware*,
All things to enjoy and regret.

Negate somewhere in between and be happy.

Glenn Freeth

Tears

What can I say to tell you
That I can understand your loss;
I have no words to take away your pain.

What can I offer to bring hope
And strength and consolation;
What words to ease your sorrow.

I struggle to bring comfort in some way,
To help you through the darkness
And I can offer nothing but my tears.

E Shirley Whitman

NUMBER 7

The orange doors of
the cottage, black
velvet squares on
the front. The windows
all closed with the
curtains drawn, eyes
peering out that
are curious. Eyes
that cannot see,
that have dreamed
but not woken up
yet. The windblown
painted stone blocks
they are constructed from
have begun to crumble,
the minds
that once held
them together have
now grown decadent.

Jason Roycroft

A Journey

As I was sitting
supping strong lager
which went straight
to my head,
I wondered if
the brain
would feel much the same,
when floating
through outer space,
in a capsule
with one large oval window.
There are two yearnings
which never leave the mind.
One is to seek out
the soul.
Hail bright and wondrous nature,
in all your different guises.
You bring me solace
when I am down
and my contentment
brings a faith
and an inward belief.
I yearn to
touch the stars.
Let me mingle and
caress you,
in the dark and
silent world of the spheres,
for you are my crystal friends
who have travelled
throughout the years.

Tom Clarke

JELLY BEANS

I promised myself long ago that when you come here
I'll straighten that crooked picture. The one depicting
a single tree, blown and bowed by Irish wind. Squashed
in a brick bracelet of houses like a bleached charm,

my home will not be what you are used to. I suspect
you are all drawing rooms and drapes, not merry
woodchip. I fear your strong sense of aesthetics may
be affronted by cracked lino and wobbly cupboards,

not to mention the layer of dust on the partly stripped
skirting boards. I'll tackle the grill pan and defrost
something tasteful. I could light candles, in the gloom
you won't notice pine needles, six months old, still

held prisoner by the carpets nylon hooks, and the cobwebs
should hide themselves nicely in the shadows.
My books might impress, as long as you don't study
the pile on the bathroom floor, all cheap anthologies

and spiritual self-help. I'll polish my shoes, and put
on something smart, not designer you understand,
a floaty frock from the High Street. I promise myself
that when you come here I'll straighten that picture.

The crooked one, that has hung forever on the sliding
hands of time, and when I do, the stitching around my
mouth will unravel, allowing all the secrets to come
tumbling out, like jelly beans into the dish of your hands.

Victoria Buckley

BY MY SIDE

Just knowing you were there,
That someone loved me,
Someone cared,
To know that you were eternally by my side.
But now that you are gone,
Something in my life
Is wrong,
I see an empty space right by my side.

You were always there for me,
On you I could rely,
You knew my every problem,
Saw through my every lie.
And how I wish you were now by my side.
To say you've gone just sounds so weird,
It was the one thing
That I feared
That you would not be always by my side.

Now memories are all I have to keep,
Though in spirit you guard me,
Through waking and sleep,
But you are not right there by my side.
You will stay forever in my thoughts,
Both when I'm happy,
When I'm sad or distraught
Your spirit will stay by my side.

Ceryn Rowntree

WHEN IT ALL ADDS UP

To quantify the situation.
Divide the mistakes.
Multiply the reasons why.
Protract the right angle.
Measure the cost.
Subtract the precise information.
Average out the pros and cons.
Equate the ideas.
Draw the line between right and wrong.
Symmetrical similarities appear.
Rhomboid the sound of silence.
Conclusions form with positive certainty.

Do the sum, give a response,
But only when it all adds up.

Anne Melling

INFORMATION

We hope you have enjoyed reading this book - and that you will continue to enjoy it in the coming years.

If you like reading and writing poetry drop us a line, or give us a call, and we'll send you a free information pack.

Write to :-
    Poetry Now Information
    1-2 Wainman Road
    Woodston
    Peterborough
    PE2 7BU
    (01733) 230746